D1452015

U2's *THE JOSHUA TREE*

U2's *The Joshua Tree*

Planting Roots in Mythic America

Bradley Morgan

Backbeat
Books

Guilford, Connecticut

Backbeat Books

An imprint of Globe Pequot, the trade division of
The Rowman & Littlefield Publishing Group, Inc.
4501 Forbes Blvd., Ste. 200
Lanham, MD 20706
www.rowman.com

Distributed by NATIONAL BOOK NETWORK

British Library Cataloguing in Publication Information available

Library of Congress Cataloging-in-Publication Data

Names: Morgan, Bradley, author.
Title: U2's the Joshua tree : planting roots in mythic America / Bradley
  Morgan.
Description: Guilford, Connecticut : Backbeat, 2021. | Includes
  bibliographical references and index. | Summary: "The book is an
  examination of the social and political origins of U2's 1987 album The
  Joshua Tree, contextualized amid our current political climate" —Provided by publisher.
Identifiers: LCCN 2021023882 (print) | LCCN 2021023883 (ebook) | ISBN
  9781493061174 (cloth) | ISBN 9781493061181 (epub)
Subjects: LCSH: U2 (Musical group). Joshua tree. | Rock music—Political
  aspects—History—20th century. | Rock music—Political aspects—United
  States—History—21st century. | Rock music—1981–1990—History and
  criticism.
Classification: LCC ML421.U2 M67 2021 (print) | LCC ML421.U2 (ebook) |
  DDC 782.42166092/2—dc23
LC record available at https://lccn.loc.gov/2021023882
LC ebook record available at https://lccn.loc.gov/2021023883

♾️™ The paper used in this publication meets the minimum requirements of American
National Standard for Information Sciences—Permanence of Paper for Printed Library
Materials, ANSI/NISO Z39.48-1992.

Contents

FOREWORD

The Fire This Time

THERE ARE MOVIES THAT IN ESSENCE YOU'VE SEEN WITHOUT HAVING actually seen. At least, that's what you tell yourself. You catch scenes here and there when channel surfing, or maybe it's on TV behind the bar or in the background somewhere. If you're the kind of cinephile that pays attention to these sort of things, you actually keep track of the bits you've caught over time, even when they only register in your periphery. You mentally file these clips away like stray puzzle pieces or spare parts, someday connecting them to other bits and either solving the title you couldn't figure out and/or checking another off your list. In some cases, these splinters may be the only relationship you have with a particular movie.

In fact, though, you've only "frankenseen" these movies: you caught bloody chunks out of sequence, some sections repeated, others missing, some with the volume muted, and so on. You've preconstructed the plot based on what you've picked up over time, but in fact, you're robbing the film of the contexts in which those portions were designed to live. And as most narratives are constructed with clues and hints in one scene paying off in another, fragmentary viewing does nobody any favors. And yet at some point, we all fall into the trap of determining that what you've seen is enough to know that it isn't worth investing serious time and energy. We've all done it; no shame to be had.

Over the years I had heard most of the songs from *The Joshua Tree* but never actually played the album from start to finish. Now, it would be one thing if it were one of the thousands of albums I was born too late to be there for originally, but as a high school senior when it came out, I have no excuse. The album was everywhere, bleeding from almost every pair of headphones within earshot. At that point in my life, I was only a part-time U2 fan. I liked songs here and there, wasn't moved by others, and essentially didn't mind them being around but never dove into their catalog like I did with the artists I was really into. My musical path at the time had me down more off-beat roads, and it was easy, too easy, to write off U2 as too mainstream for me (not that there's anything wrong with that).

Fast forward four years and the band dropped "The Fly" single from *Achtung Baby*. Suddenly, I heard a dark and mysterious U2 I'd never heard of before, one conjuring a postmodern vibe and infusing electronica into their sound. Some U2 purists decried this new direction as U2 2.0, but it seduced me head over heels, and suddenly I couldn't wait for the next single and the sundry of remixes that came with them.

That said, it never occurred to me to catch up with their catalog like I would for other artists, searching for hints in their formative years of the later magic that ultimately roped me in. No, as far as I was concerned, this new sound was miles if not planets away from "Where the Streets Have No Name," "I Still Haven't Found What I'm Looking For," and others. Eno or no Eno, what could those albums possibly do for me?

Or so I convinced myself.

As with those movies only frankenseen, context and continuity matter when it comes to albums. Singles are chosen to both stand on their own and offer a glimpse into the larger work from which they were born. And like movies, albums are conceived (and usually delivered) as complete experiences if not actual statements. No one would dream of looking at a 6" × 6" cutout of Pablo Picasso's *Guernica* and conclude that they "get" the entire painting; but it's a slippery slope when it comes to movies and music. And in a culture that seems determined to compartmentalize both statements and experiences, it becomes a challenge to process and appreciate the greater artistic intent of works demanding time and attention.

With all that baggage, I sat down with *The Joshua Tree* now, 33 years after the world was first enchanted by it, and expected that, at best, it'd be better than I thought and I would realize my folly in blowing it off all these years. What I didn't expect was to really like the album I heard. I assumed that its holy trinity of singles ("With or Without You," "I Still Haven't Found What I'm Looking For," and "Where the Streets Have No Name") was the best the album had to offer. Giving it the proper listen it deserved, it became a private time warp and a connection to something timeless all at once.

The year 1987 didn't start like a particularly exciting one in terms of new music. The initial buzz over the massive live boxset by Bruce Springsteen and Stevie Ray Vaughan's *Live Alive*, both released in the final months of 1986, had already faded. A new album from Prince was due in March, something cool to look forward to, for sure. The Beastie Boys' debut was a polarizing beast, drawing accusations of misogyny and "unethical" sampling (because even for people who didn't like rap music or care about black-on-black sampling, slicing and dicing Led Zeppelin was a cardinal sin). It was a cold winter, musically speaking, which made it perfect for an album like *The Joshua Tree* to take the world by storm.

Ronald Reagan had already provided much fodder for popular and alternative music. The Clash called out US intervention in Latin America with *Sandinista!* at the dawn of the decade. In 1983, the

Rolling Stones delivered their first overtly political song in years with "Undercover of the Night," evoking corruption and death squads in no small order. And 1984, the year of Ronnie's reelection, saw the release of two era-defining classics: Frankie Goes to Hollywood's damnation of Cold War politics, "Two Tribes," and the gonzoid "5 Minutes," a one-off collaboration between Jerry Harrison and Bootsy Collins that sampled a recording of Reagan joking off-air that nuclear annihilation was imminent (the infamous "We begin bombing in five minutes"). Global politics inspired collective protest actions in the middle of the decade, targeting South African apartheid (the "Sun City" single) and famine relief in Africa (the Live Aid concert).

Politics was no stranger to popular music at the time, but it was usually worn on its sleeve (figuratively and sometimes literally). Any casual fan or listener who picked up *The Joshua Tree* on the basis of its radio-friendly calling cards was in for a major surprise: governmental tyranny, global imperialism, religious hypocrisy, labor struggles, drug addiction, and so on. The lovesick "With or Without You" fades, and listeners are thrust into the fever-dream delirium that is "Bullet the Blue Sky," an open letter to the world decrying US intervention in El Salvador. It ends with a mic drop and is followed by the soft and delicate opening of "Running to Stand Still," a poignant portrait of drug addiction in an Irish apartment complex. What an exhausting first side for vinyl listeners (although *The Joshua Tree* was apparently one of the first albums conceived as a continuous whole for the then-new CD format, its side A/side B dynamic is still brilliantly constructed).

This album could have come out today: its questions and callouts are as spot-on as they were 33 years ago. At times I almost have to remind myself that it is that old. The red-faced devil of "Bullet the Blue Sky" could as easily have been throwing money and the military at Afghanistan and Northern Africa as it did to El Salvador and Latin America.

Today's average listener probably knows someone firsthand who took the poison in "Running to Stand Still" and floated away forever. For all the album's timelessness in our culture, we might all have preferred that some of the lyrics had faded rather than endured.

Cynics point to Bono's jet-setting world tours of impoverished and war-torn areas as self-serving or, in the worst criticisms, leftist moralizing. And to be fair, *The Joshua Tree* probably is the most, if not the *only* political album on any Top 10 list it makes. When you think of politically motivated songs, they tend to be didactic—rattling off facts, often in the form of rhetorical questions—or overly narrative, handheld storytelling from an omniscient third person. But Bono doesn't actually preach or moralize in the lyrics. The album's perspective is pointedly personal, and at times, Bono's portrait of the duality of the United States feels like we're eavesdropping on someone's inner dialogue. The band has been staunchly unambiguous, however, about the album's political statement in interviews since its release.

The Joshua Tree was the first big album of 1987. *Sign 'O' The Times*, *Appetite for Destruction*, the *Dirty Dancing* soundtrack, *Bad*, and *Faith* would all follow before the year was over. All have survived the ensuing decades and do better to define the 1980s than much of the music that most listeners would agree embody the classic 1980s style, but *The Joshua Tree* might be the ballsiest of the bunch. With the sweeping grace of its major singles out of the way, the rest of the album is unafraid to bring ugly truths front and center, flowing from one to the next like a world tour of pain and angst by magic carpet ride. Bold, elegant, gutsy, and poetic, beguiling in its delivery, and unabashed in its message.

At this writing, the world still waits to see what changes the transition out of a Donald J. Trump regime will have on the world. Bono's lyrics might still leave an indelible footprint on the collective psyche of fans new and old. We can only hope that its political messages become time capsules as the misguided ethics of imperialism, fundamentalism, and total-itarianism become historical footnotes instead of front-page headlines.

—Gregor Meyer
December 2020

Writer-at-large Gregor Meyer is a counterculture musicologist, film historian, and lifelong record collector. His writing appears in the online magazine *Perfect Sound Forever* and in *Fellini: The Sixties*, published by Running Press. Meyer was also the lead researcher for biographies of actors Peter Sellers (*Mr. Strangelove*, Hyperion, 2002) and Bette Davis (*Dark Victory*, Henry Holt, 2007). When not listening to music, writing about it, or digging through record crates, he cohosts the film review podcast *Hollywood Rx*.

ACKNOWLEDGMENTS

THIS BOOK STARTED OUT AS A LABOR OF LOVE, AND I WAS FORTUNATE to be surrounded by so much love throughout the project. Authoring a book is quite a challenging undertaking. There were moments throughout the process that I had felt so amazing about the work and there were moments that I had my doubts. During the time I spent conceptualizing the book, writing it, and pitching it, I received such valuable guidance and feedback from friends, colleagues, and experts. I firmly believe that no one is an island. We are only as good as the company we keep, and I deeply appreciate the company I have kept and those who have kept me. I feel so rich because of them. This book belongs to them just as much as it does to me because I am unsure if I could have finished it the way I had envisioned without them. I received so much great advice and support on areas such as writing, marketing, development, publishing, and other essentials to get a project like this off the ground, and of course their emotional support. Thank you so much to Farah Ali, Steven Anderson, Ellen Barkenbush, Michael Bennett, Paul Birza, Andy Bugay, Scott Calhoun, Rene Calvo, Patrick Collins, Mary Conway, Jessi DiBartolomeo, Juliann Esqueda, Gary Fraser, Josh Friedberg, Al Gabor, Holly Hanson, Joe Held, Lee Herman, Karen Johnson, Carolyn Kassnoff, Alex Kemmler, Debra LaRocco, Jennifer Lizak, Ari Maduff, Jean Mahony, Abby Matt, Amanda Mayo, Dan Menna, Mike Nikolich, Nicole Oppenheim, Kyle Sanders, Eric Sinclair, Joe Stewart,

Barry Talbert, Amelia Vargas, Eric Wiersema, Simmon Yoon, Anne Zender, and Cynthia Zender.

When I started the book, the original vision was a bit different than how it would turn out. While I was still in the early stages of how I wanted to craft the narrative, Rebecca Suzan graciously offered her expertise and support as a copyeditor for the proposal and outline. With her input, advice, and even some push and pull on some details, I was able to figure out what I wanted to say and in the best way possible. I became a much better writer because of Rebecca, and I am eternally grateful for her guidance.

I am thankful for Gregor Meyer for authoring the foreword. Gregor is an incredibly talented and gifted writer, so it meant so much to me when he accepted the offer to contribute to my book. I was incredibly moved that he was able to capture the spirit and essence of my narrative through his own perspective. The breadth of Gregor's musical and cultural knowledge is so vast and his ideas so incredibly insightful that it was an absolute honor to have him involved.

I am incredibly grateful to Globe Pequot Press, Backbeat Books, and Rowman & Littlefield. My deepest and sincerest gratitude goes to John Cerullo for accepting my manuscript, guiding me during my first time through the publishing process, and working with me to make it the best possible book I could deliver. Many thanks to Carol Flannery, Barbara Claire, and Ashleigh Cooke at Rowman & Littlefield for their support preparing the book for publishing. And, of course, thank you to Claudia Gravier Frigo for her superb copyediting support.

And, most importantly, I express my endless thanks and gratitude to my family. Without them, nothing in my life would be possible. Their love is the greatest gift of all, and I would not be who I am without them. Thank you, and I love you.

Chapter One

Outside Is America

On Christmas Day 2016, less than two months after Donald J. Trump became the president-elect of the United States, U2 released a video on their website as a message to their fans announcing their plans for the coming year. As the Edge played the melody from "Little Drummer Boy" on guitar in his classic effects-laden style, and Adam Clayton was decorating a Joshua tree in the traditional style of a Christmas tree including ornaments and tinsel while Larry Mullen Jr. showed off an electronic dancing Santa, Bono announced 2017 would be an exciting year for the band highlighting the release of a new album and, in anticipation of its 30th anniversary, some special shows to celebrate their landmark 1987 album *The Joshua Tree*. The lights came down as the band left the scene and the image of a Joshua tree, glowing with a festive spirit, was left to entice and tease fans as to what would unfold over the next year. [U2.com, "Happy Christmas"]

U2's original plan to celebrate the 30th anniversary of *The Joshua Tree* was to commemorate the anniversary with a single show in the United States and Europe each. That plan would soon evolve into a full tour because the band recognized that the themes of *The Joshua Tree*, composed as a critique of the United States under Ronald Reagan's presidential administration, were still relevant amid the authoritarian and populist principles of Trump, which were an extremist appropriation of Reagan's neoconservative policies. In an interview with Andy Greene for *Rolling Stone*, The Joshua Tree Tour 2017's set designer Willie Williams said that the tour was not about rehashing the original Joshua Tree tour. As opposed to touring the album purely for nostalgic reasons, the 30th anniversary tour would include elements on a reflection of the album's modern relevance despite being inspired and written as a response to the era of Reagan and Margaret Thatcher. For the band, it felt as if history was repeating itself. [Greene, "U2's Longtime Stage Designer"]

Trump's election and his promises of enforcing policies that emboldened white nationalism and supremacy were a turning point for U2. Though they were working to progress forward as a band, they could not ignore the connections Trump had to their past. The Edge, in conversation with Andy Greene for *Rolling Stone*, discussed the election's impact saying that he felt that Trump's win signified a reversal. With Trump, policies and rhetoric that fueled social and political instability they had addressed in the album originally, such as the violent interventions in Central America and the UK miners' strike, had returned. Trump's brand of populism and penchant for authoritarianism reignited unrest that felt similar to what the band had addressed three decades prior. The Edge recalled that the band had not experienced any of their other albums resonating in such a way that the songs continued to gain a newer and modern significance that they did not have initially. [Greene, "The Edge"]

In developing the concept for The Joshua Tree Tour 2017, the Edge explained that U2 had to reconsider how to approach their music differently from before. Throughout their career, they had never sought to observe their own musical past as a band. Instead, they always sought to move forward as a band artistically and musically, undergoing several aesthetic and sonic reinventions. The surprising relevance of *The Joshua Tree* in this modern context gave them pause to consider the possibility of celebrating their past for the first time. The 30th anniversary tour became an opportune moment to reflect on their accomplished album and reconsider how they approached their own history as a band. In a way, given the album's relevance under Trump, looking back to the past became a way to explore just how far U2 had come since 1987, but at the same time understanding that new life breathed into their music could move them forward. [Greene, "The Edge"]

During the 2016 presidential campaign, prior to the 2017 tour, U2 had been lambasting Trump during live performances. On October 5, 2016, one month prior to the election, they performed at Salesforce's Dreamforce conference with a fiery, political set that highlighted the importance of recognizing the danger US democracy faced under the threat of a Trump presidency. During a performance of "Bullet the Blue Sky," images of Trump appeared on the projection screen with Bono, via megaphone, asking him if the wall he wanted to build, the one along the United States–Mexico border, was really meant to be a wall like the Berlin Wall or the Great Wall of China, which were symbols of isolation and divisiveness. Bono continued by asking if what Trump said by "making America great again," he actually meant making America hate again, contextualizing Trump's campaign slogan as a call to enforce racial, ethnic, and cultural prejudice.

At the iHeartRadio Festival the week prior, U2 played "Desire," from *Rattle and Hum*, with Bono rhetorically asking the audience what they would be willing to lose. He asked if they were ready to gamble away their house and the American Dream, in response to a repeating video of Trump asking "What do you have to lose?" intercut with images of money, gambling, and bright casino lights, closing with an emphasized clip of Trump declaring "the American Dream is dead." [Bhattacharjee, "You're Fired"]

Throughout the 2016 campaign, even off stage, U2 were vocal about the threat Trump posed to US democracy. In an interview with

Charlie Rose in September 2016, Bono was candid about Trump and his potential impact on US citizens and their freedoms. Championing the ideals that America represented to him, Bono said that Trump could devastate those ideals. For Bono, America represented the greatest idea in the history of the world, but that Trump could possibly be the worst thing to ever happen to it. [Rose, interview]

The members of U2 grew up in Ireland and had an intimate attachment to America. For them, and many previous generations of Irish people, America meant freedom from famine and poverty, as well as new opportunities to prosper. U2 were well aware of their country's connection to America and the hand that Irish immigrants had in building America as it exists today. And yet, through the journey of recording *The Joshua Tree*, the band would come to understand that the reality of America did not match the myth they grew up with that heralds it as a refuge. Therefore, it was important to work toward the ideals of what America had meant to them and could mean to people 30 years after recording their landmark album. In his interview with Rose, Bono expressed that America represented more than just a country to him; it represented an idea founded on the principle of equal justice for everyone. [Rose, interview]

U2 were critical of Trump months prior to the election, but after his election, The Joshua Tree Tour 2017 would be the band's platform to modernize the themes of *The Joshua Tree* as a message that not only critiqued the existential crisis Trump posed to America but also called for the bridging of the country's divisions. Despite comments from U2 on Trump during interviews, the space established for the tour would focus on the positive messages inherent in *The Joshua Tree* as a means to unite people impacted by the US dichotomy. It became essential, in contrast with the hateful rhetoric spewed by Trump, for U2 to talk about the American Dream as a concept that everyone, regardless of political party affiliation or racial, ethnic, and national background, could share instead of being institutionally dismantled for certain people by Trump. Though U2 had been critical of Trump, their comments were not an indictment of those manipulated by him. During the US leg of the tour, The Joshua Tree Tour 2017 was a space for all people to unite for a common national idea based on the beliefs and principles U2 had of America growing up. During an interview on *Jimmy Kimmel Live*, Bono expanded on this idea saying that U2 worked with everyone when it came to complex political and social matters. If the dialogue was held between those with conservative or liberal ideals, U2 were focused on finding a commonality, one thing that people could agree on, because that would serve as the foundation for a constructive conversation. [Kimmel, interview]

Continuing on this point during the Kimmel interview, Bono acknowledged how different things were with the Trump administration than under previous administrations. For Bono, things in America had changed, and he felt a level of respect and understanding for the Americans who voted for Trump. Their motivation to support Trump came from a place of anger regarding their country, an anger that Bono could relate to having grown up when Ireland was troubled by poverty and other social issues. Bono empathized with their disillusionment with politics and government, and their believing that the whole system was too fractured to function in a way that would alleviate their deepest concerns and grievances. However, despite this understanding, Bono expressed that Trump was not the solution to their problems and that he would, in fact, make things worse. For U2, Trump did not have the interests of the American people in mind but, rather, was motivated by his own self-interests. Although Trump liked to see the massive crowds at his rallies, Bono felt that Trump did not respect the same people when they left and returned home. [Kimmel, interview]

While the themes of *The Joshua Tree* were proving to be relevant three decades after its initial release, U2 realized that the stakes were much higher under Trump. Trump's success as a presidential candidate came from his savvy ability to use media as a weapon to stoke peoples' fears. Although such a practice is not new within politics, Trump came at the right time with his own brand of populism to capitalize on the unrest many Americans had felt over the last decade, often distressed by their lack of economic and social progress. Many Americans were feeling frustrated and vulnerable, and the conditions were right for a potential demagogue to come and take advantage of the situation. Bono, recognizing the shift toward distrust in US political institutions, said too many people, both liberal and conservative, had lost faith in their government and its ability to functionally operate. As a result, this animosity toward the political process created a new kind of constituency, one that was distrustful of political institutions, which could be easily manipulated by figures like Trump. Bono told Greene that it becomes easy for people to become bullies after being bullied for so long, a coping mechanism for the grievances they felt. Bono described it as them reacting to a lost innocence which represented a critical moment in the history of America. [Greene, "Bono on How"]

Despite its flaws, U2 remained adamant about celebrating America and upholding their belief of the country's founding principles of liberty and justice for all. At a concert in Detroit during The Joshua Tree Tour 2017, Bono expressed to the audience that America represented a second home to the band. For them, America was less a country and more of an idea and that they wanted this idea to succeed. With the admonition of America to get out of its own way, the bright ideas the country promised could become a brighter reality. [U2, Detroit concert] This idea of America, as U2 believed, is one "that belongs to people who need it most," a notion built on the belief that collectively working toward fulfilling the promise of America was essential in order to end the inequality for those most at risk over America's failure to keep its promise. [Inskeep, "U2"]

The Joshua Tree Tour 2017 was a unique opportunity for the band to explore the past in order to influence, musically and politically, the future for themselves and others who could be impacted by a racist and nationalist American policy. In a time where legacy acts, such as U2, could rest on their laurels and play their most famous songs or albums as is, it is rare that a band considers the timeliness of their work and assesses, if possible, its modern relevance. Contextualizing *The Joshua Tree* amid the political crisis under Trump, U2 provided audiences with a guiding framework on how they could change things for the better. It was as if to say that, although this democratic crisis was unlike anything modern Americans had seen before, its citizens still had the power to protect the promise of democracy as a reality more accessible than ever before.

I attended the first of two performances of The Joshua Tree Tour 2017 at Soldier Field in Chicago with my dad. Attending this concert was exciting for both of us because this was his first U2 concert, and I was turning 30 that year, the same milestone as *The Joshua Tree*, which we, as well as all the other concertgoers, were celebrating. We had planned to go together for months, and I kept him up to date on all the news and surprises that had unfurled during the previous performances.

My dad and I have varying, and often conflicting, political views. He is a conservative who voted for Trump during the 2016 presidential election, whereas I supported Bernie Sanders during the primary before transferring that support to Hillary Clinton for the general election. When I saw U2 speak about Trump online or read quotes criticizing his administration, I got a little anxious about the concert before the tour even started. Americans were entering an extremely divisive era, and I did not want this concert, an opportunity for a father and son to share a great experience and listen to awesome music together, to make either of us feel uncomfortable, or like a target, for the differences in our political views. I had to trust that U2 would make a definitive point but with a tone that matched their universal appeal. They did the job splendidly, and my dad and I had a great time, bonding over the band's message of commonality and humanism through the lens of America's promised ideals.

I had been more politically active than I ever had before, up to that point, largely because of the threat Trump posed to democracy, so I appreciated the critique inherent in *The Joshua Tree* and the lessons that could be applied in a modern context 30 years later in concert. Through my eyes and experiences, America began a fall from grace as a democratic leader when it began to flirt with, and even adopt, authoritarian, fascist, and populist policies and ideals in a mainstream way when they had primarily existed in the margins of political extremism in the past (though to many older and Black, indigenous, and people of color [BIPOC] Americans, this fall from grace is much older or even inherent in the nation's founding). However, *The Joshua Tree* helped me connect my experiences with those during the Reagan era when the album was being recorded. This reflected Trump's coopting of Reagan's principles but in a way that elevated his notion of turning America, from a perceived multicultural promised land, to a fundamentalist white-ethno state where the wealthy elite ruled.

History does often repeat itself and will continue to do so. Going to that performance of The Joshua Tree Tour 2017 really opened up my eyes to what exactly *The Joshua Tree* was saying about America and my cultural identity. U2 had typically included ideas of politics in their music, and I knew *The Joshua Tree* was no exception. However, I had not fully grasped the nuance of the album until that point. *The Joshua Tree* was not just a collection of songs but rather a vibrant idea about the role America played in U2's lives and the role they believed the country could play in the lives of its own citizens. I knew that America had its own inherent flaws within systems that influenced disparity in the country, but I often did not have hope and I became bitter and angry toward how America often treated marginalized people. *The Joshua Tree* instilled in me an optimism and realization that Americans need their country to be the promised land it had historically claimed to be, and the conviction that the nation was at its best when everyone was free from disparity it perpetuates. Even during times as dark as the Trump era, there is an urgency for America to become unified and bridge the gap of its own dichotomy.

Despite the progress that had occurred during the last three decades since their first existential journey through America, U2 recognized that America's dichotomy was growing. With an admonishment toward America regarding the rise of fascism and authoritarianism under Trump during this tour, U2 would go on a second, more mature, existential journey through the American heartland to find the beauty Americans thought they had lost. To go on that journey with U2, I would have to look to their past, as well as my own, to see firsthand how they discovered, for themselves, the two Americas.

Chapter Two

The Two Americas

When U2 performed at Live Aid on July 13, 1985, they were playing to their biggest audience ever to date. Performing for more than 72,000 attendees at Wembley Stadium and broadcasting to an estimated 1.9 billion people in more than 150 nations, vocalist Bono, guitarist the Edge, drummer Larry Mullen Jr., and bassist Adam Clayton would soon be catapulted to rock stardom as members of one of the biggest bands in the world. Though the band had performed in smaller clubs and theaters throughout America over the last few years, U2 were now, as *Time* put it, "rock's hottest ticket" [*Time*, "Rock's Hottest Ticket"] and were introduced to US audiences on a scale they never achieved before. U2 would soon be greeted by swarms of fans as they toured and performed in stadiums and arenas across America, giving them a platform to share their beliefs and insights throughout the land of the free. Motivated to capitalize on this new success, they set out to make their next album a reflection of their experiences touring America, as well as their increasing awareness of the country's culture and politics. Released on March 9, 1987, *The Joshua Tree* would be U2's critique of America through the eyes of foreigners and its inherent dichotomy between the American Dream and the American Reality.

Growing up in Ireland, the members of U2 had an intimate attachment to America. Reflecting on this in an interview with Michka Assayas, Bono said, "The Irish came over from a death culture, of famine, and of colonization, which of course was emasculation. They found a new virility in America. They began a new life in America. And this of course is at the heart of the idea of redemption: to begin again." [Assayas, *Bono*, 188] Though, as U2 wrote and recorded *The Joshua Tree*, the band would soon discover that their understanding of America was one based on a myth. In an interview with *National Public Radio*, Bono described the role America played in their lives as kids in Ireland, saying, "We were obsessed by America at the time. America's a sort of promised land for Irish people— and then, a sort of potentially broken promised land." [Inskeep, "U2"]

For inspiration on the direction of U2's follow-up to 1984's *The Unforgettable Fire*, an album with varying abstract musical elements and themes, Bono urged the band to explore the complexities of America through its culture and heartland by crafting a cohesive musical and narrative theme to reflect that. Bono became fascinated with American literature, reading works by authors such as Truman Capote and Norman Mailer. He had also recently become aware of the role that Reagan's foreign policy, through military interventions throughout Central and South America, played in benefitting the cause of his Christian fundamentalist supporters. There was a thread of violence and darkness throughout these elements of the United States that Bono observed and he felt compelled to examine them in relation to his own self. [McCormick and U2, *U2 by U2*, 184]

Originally with the working title *The Two Americas*, what would eventually result in *The Joshua Tree* was U2, as Bono reflected, beginning to "see two Americas, the mythic and the real America." [McCormick and U2, *U2 by U2*, 177] The album would address the darkness Bono recognized within the reality of America that impacted the concept of the American Dream as perceived by its own citizens and foreigners, who, like U2 in Ireland, had believed America to be a promised land. The Edge echoed the rest of the band's feelings about America in *U2 by U2*, saying that the dream of America championed by Martin Luther King Jr., as opposed to its depiction in the media, enchanted the band. King's vision, along with the American literature Bono was reading as well as the country's cinematic landscape, held an appeal for the band that became a source of inspiration and a springboard for them to explore America as an idea. [McCormick and U2, *U2 by U2*, 177]

As U2 embarked on their existential journey through the complex tapestry of hypocrisies and ideals that was America, they recognized that they had to conceptualize their music in a way they had not done before. U2 had dabbled with a lot of experimentation and breaking new ground, according to the Edge, when recording *The Unforgettable Fire*. For their follow-up album, which would become *The Joshua Tree*, they wanted to work with a different process that was more reliant on establishing boundaries to achieve a specific vision. Their goal became to write songs that were intended to be less ambiguous and more focused, creating a clear and succinct vision for what they wanted to express about America. [Stokes, *Into the Heart*, 66]

Recording an album that would be conceptually more focused in its atmosphere than their previous album, U2 relied on the American landscape to give the album a cinematic quality. During a discussion with Brian Eno, coproducer for *The Joshua Tree* alongside Daniel Lanois, the desert as a concept for the album would frequently come up. Out of these conversations, the Edge said the American Southwest, with its arid and bone-dry deserts, served as the image influencing the album's lyrics, acting as the set backdrop for their cinematic vision of America's dichotomy. According to the Edge in *Classic Albums*, this cinematic quality of *The Joshua Tree* was to draw inspiration from the American landscape and craft an album that transported the listener to the places U2 had explored. [*Classic Albums, The Joshua Tree*]

Bono was certainly attracted to the desert as a theme for *The Joshua Tree* because much of the literature he was reading took place in the American heartlands of the Midwest and Southwest. The desert, with its symbolic properties as a brutal landscape with a hidden beauty, reflected Bono's struggle with identity and his perception of America. During the recording sessions, the desert became a place of fascination for U2. For Bono, the desert as an inspiration resulted in him thinking deeply about his own identity, who he was as a person, and how he felt his life was unbalanced emotionally. This self-reflection eventually allowed him to become aware of what he was witnessing and to develop his songwriting to comment on his adoration of America as well as his fear of how much worse it could be. [McCormick and U2, *U2 by U2*, 177]

Enhancing the songs' narrative themes on *The Joshua Tree* that critiqued the hypocrisies of America, the desert's stark imagery presented the perfect backdrop for U2's critique of America and the spirit of its people. On the imagery of the desert, and the journey early American settlers embarked on to reach their promised land and the struggles they endured, the Edge said, "The desert is a transitional place. It doesn't have a kind of right or wrong, nor any kind of strong personality. For us, it was like a journey through this neutral ground to get to where we were going." [McCormick and U2, *U2 by U2*, 186]

For Bono, credited as *The Joshua Tree*'s sole lyricist, it became important to write lyrics that, unlike on previous records, reflected his own personal encounters with the two distinct Americas. To write these songs, Bono had to figure out how to convey his experience with America while reconciling his own feelings about America when he was growing up in Ireland with what he came to realize as he explored it when writing *The Joshua Tree*. [Stokes, "The World About Us"] Many of the songs, during writing and recording for *The Joshua Tree*, would be influenced by his humanitarian missions in Ethiopia, El Salvador, and Nicaragua, where he would witness firsthand the effects of America's foreign policy and how it differed from the messaging Americans would receive from the Reagan administration.

As much as *The Joshua Tree* reflected U2's existential journey through America, an exploration of the country's dichotomy as a critique of its foreign and domestic policies, the album also reflected the band's personal journey of self-discovery. During the recording of *The Joshua Tree*, the band would undergo struggles, both personal and artistic, that shaped the development of the album, which also gave them an opportunity to reflect on changes in their lives and within their own individual identities. Through obstacles such as marriage issues, the death of a friend, and even being forced to reevaluate how to approach their art, America challenged U2 in ways they had not experienced before, requiring reflection and searching for salvation during their journey. On U2's own national identity, the Edge said that the band did not fully understand the breadth and scope of their own Irishness until they left Ireland and explored America, feeling a sense of alienation by the experience. [Irwin, "This Is What We Do Best"]

Though *The Joshua Tree* would condemn America for its hypocritical policies that devastated foreign lands and denied its own citizens fair and equal access to the American Dream, U2 still admired America for the idea it had meant to them growing up and what it could still mean. On this distinction between admonishing and admiring America, Larry said that U2 had a "love/hate relationship with America" and that the album's name represented how U2 were influenced by American culture. For aspiring bands in Ireland during the 1970s, America was not only the hippest place to be, but it was also the only way to break out of Ireland because it had the biggest music sales and touring markets. The UK music press routinely ignored Irish bands, so America became the focus for U2 to further their career. Larry expressed that America had welcomed them in a way that was completely unexpected for them and that this to him represented an openness and freedom in America. For

U2, this relationship with America, fueled by their perceptions growing up in Ireland and trying to break out of their home country as a musical act, was the basis for tribute and evaluation within *The Joshua Tree*. "We weren't looking for *The Joshua Tree*," according to Larry, "*The Joshua Tree* came looking for us." [McCormick and U2, *U2 by U2,* 186]

Despite the two Americas U2 would discover during their existential journey recording *The Joshua Tree*, there was much to cherish about the country. Although the album reflected the American dichotomy being maintained, or even enhanced, through the exploitation of the country's inherently flawed institutions, U2 recognized there was a deeply rooted drive within the people to prosper. It was the same drive that they saw in their own country's history.

For Bono, one of the qualities of America he cherished was that it was a place where one could reinvent oneself. Much in the spirit of U2 always looking forward with their music, the vision they had for America was less about the past but rather the destination. This journeying concept, for Bono, represented the foundational aspect of the American Dream. [Assayas, *Bono*, 188] As they embarked on their journey through America to record *The Joshua Tree*, overcoming doubt, anguish, fear, and even death, U2 would be reinvented by their experience, stronger in conscience and expression. *The Joshua Tree* would be their admonishment and celebration of a country that could again begin to make the American Dream the American Reality.

CHAPTER THREE

Tree of Pain

WITHIN THE HALLOWED HALLS OF HOLY WORSHIP, A REGAL FIGURE was emblazoned on the walls. This divine being gazed on the flock with knowing eyes that revealed contempt. Gilded with sovereign glory, he moved swiftly on those who committed sin against his kingdom. With wrath straight from the Old Testament, he exacts his righteous fury.

"Wow, what's Ronald Reagan doing there on the chariot?" Bono asked. Standing in the middle of a church in a village in El Salvador, Bono was staring at a mural depicting the US president portrayed as the Pharaoh of the Old Testament. "We are the children of Israel running away," someone replied. [Inskeep, "U2"]

It was July 1986, and U2 were taking a break from recording *The Joshua Tree*. They had just completed the short, six-show A Conspiracy of Hope benefit tour in the United States on behalf of Amnesty International. Inspired by the organization's mission to raise awareness of human rights issues, Bono and his wife Ali Hewson embarked on a mission to El Salvador to see the devastation firsthand. The US intervention in the conflict between the Salvadoran military junta government and the country's citizens angered Bono. A major civil rights crisis was unfolding in Central America, aided by the greed and corruption of the Reagan administration, which supplied armaments and money.

For Reagan, the intervention was a divinely ordained mission in the ongoing effort to stop the spread of communism during the Cold War. If the album the band envisioned was going to address how America had often failed to live up to its promises, then they had to witness this firsthand. This disunion of ideals could not be explained musically by only capturing the bucolic American imagery U2 read in books and heard on records; completing the album meant facing an ugly truth.

Amid the violence committed by the Salvadoran military government's death squads, Bono had witnessed America's support for the ruling regime and the inherent hypocrisy within it. Soldiers marched through the streets, and fighter jets were seen in the air as a village over the hill was being firebombed while Bono and Ali met with US aid workers treating refugees. Back in the United States, Reagan had appealed to the burgeoning religious right movement led by Jerry Falwell and his Moral Majority. A religious movement was awakening in America, one with the sole purpose of engaging in grassroots politics to influence campaigns and elections to adopt their brand of fundamentalist Christianity.

The smiles of white, American, and Christian faces did nothing to dissuade U2 from their crusade to decry the backhanded practices of Reagan's foreign policies influenced by Falwell. "He preaches that God dresses in a three-piece polyester suit, is white, speaks in a Southern accent, is from an Anglo-Saxon background and has a wife and children," Bono said about Falwell. [Stokes, *Into the Heart*, 68] As men with deep spiritual convictions, U2's belief in a faith embodying the teachings of Jesus to aid the sick and poor were not reflected in the money-driven proclamations of the 1980s televangelists who coerced politicians to ignore human rights violations.

The ignorance of the American public, who were unaware or largely ignored the reality of these atrocities in Central America perpetrated by their government, drove U2's contempt. "People were so behind everything Ronald Reagan stood for," the Edge said. With his America First policy under the slogan "Let's Make America Great Again," Reagan wanted to resonate with the American people, so he appeared as a savior who could pull the country out of economic decline. The Edge continued, "I think when we go back to America we'll see a broken country. Either that or people refusing to look—which is more frightening." [Stokes, *Into the Heart*, 68] This was a concerning prospect given that Reagan's promises were made at the expense of dead Central Americans in favor of righteous imperialism.

The band wondered how Americans could be so blind. The people of El Salvador were fighting a brutal regime to obtain civil rights. According to Timothy D. Neufeld in *U2: Rock 'n' Roll to Change the World*, Bono felt that this fight was not unlike the struggle and violence Black men and women faced during the civil rights movement led by Dr. Martin Luther King Jr. [Neufeld, *U2*, 58] U2 had covered this territory before when they championed King as a Christ-like figure for their single "Pride (In the Name of Love)" from *The Unforgettable Fire*. Several years later, during the recording of *The Joshua Tree*, reflecting on the past was an important step U2 recognized as being integral to shaping the future. Upholding the teachings of figures like King was essential to not repeating injustices of the past, so it was troubling for the band to realize that the US government ignored its own recent history to fulfill the wants of an elite few over the needs of the many.

With the new success they found with American audiences since their Live Aid performance, U2 jumped at the opportunity to hold a mirror up to America and have the country face the injustices it was committing to serve its own needs. Bono found himself enraged by how US foreign policy was negatively impacting the lives of the citizens in El Salvador fighting for their autonomy and freedom. The money that America had funneled into their support of the oppressive Salvadoran government, paying for military equipment like planes, left Bono feeling that America was something to despise. Returning to the studio with the stark violent images of Central America fresh in his mind, Bono wanted to musically channel his experiences into the album, asking if the Edge could put "[El Salvador] through your amplifier." [McCormick, *U2 by U2*, 179]

U2 wanted to craft a song to musically reflect the heart of darkness Bono witnessed. All of the pain, blood, and suffering of the people poured out of every note in what would become the band's most angry and overtly political song to date. "Bullet the Blue Sky" was their stand against the country that recently welcomed them with open arms.

Although the lyrics came from a specific and informed experience, the music was born out of frustration and lack of cohesion. U2's primary method of recording stems from first building a musical foundation through improvised jamming, picking the pieces they like from the sessions, and then adding lyrics that complement the music. This improvisational approach that inspires and informs the songwriting is a process Bono has referred to as "sketching." [Parkyn, *Touch the Flame*, 78]

In keeping with this recording tradition and their spirit of improvisation, the demo track for "Bullet the Blue Sky" emerged from a jam session in Dublin at STS Studios and was later re-recorded and mixed at Melbeach, the Edge's home in Monkstown, a suburb in south Dublin. The band was becoming increasingly frustrated as they were performing out of sync with each other. According to *Mojo*, the Edge was working on a guitar riff while listening to The Fall, an English postpunk band founded by Mark E. Smith, and ended up with something that was "up-tempo, like real hard-hitting." Larry and Adam joined in but only playing in half-speed. Fed up, they stopped and listened to the playback and were surprised by the quality of it. For the final mix, Dave Meegan wanted to go for a Led Zeppelin feel and adjusted the monitor mix to create a heavier sound. [Eccleston, "U2"]

The severity of Bono's experience is thematically represented in the instrumentation of the song. Larry's pounding drums open the track by mimicking the heavy sound of marching boots, setting the stage for an invading sonic militia. The beats are coupled with Adam's low bass, sounding like gunfire in the distance. The fighter jets Bono witnessed thundering over the Central American jungles are recreated by a sinister drone from the Edge's guitar. Sustained for several seconds, the drone evokes jets off in the horizon that soon arrive with the sonic boom of guitar power chords. Each blasting chord embodies the jets' violent arrival and quick departure, only to repeat as if the pilots flew back around to continue their assault. You hear the carnage of El Salvador though the amplifier.

That musical onslaught sets the stage for Bono to unleash one of his most ferocious deliveries in the band's entire catalog. Bono growls as he recounts villages ravaged by violence at the hands of a country that promised to be a shining beacon of freedom in a dark world. Then he emits a guttural howl at the song's chorus as if exorcising a demon from inside, ridding himself of America's vileness. When he repeatedly cries out "bullet the blue sky," his voice oscillates between a violent declaration and a cry for mercy.

In keeping with the band's spirituality, Bono uses religious imagery in the lyrics of "Bullet the Blue Sky." Bono sings of Jacob wrestling the angel, a story from the Book of Genesis in which Jacob encounters an angel who refuses to give Jacob his name. They wrestle until daybreak, and then Jacob is blessed with the name of "Israel." Bono sings that the angel was overcome and continues with a condemnation of a demon seed being planted to raise a flower of fire. Crosses are burned, and the flames rise higher. The symbolism reflects how Bono's own spirituality exists in opposition to the practices of an American government committing violence in the name of Christianity. Bono was upset by the

cooption of religion to justify violence and brutality against those fight-
ing for their freedom and civil rights. To express how wrong this felt,
Bono relied on his faith and the Bible to write based on his experiences.
[Rock Hall and Newseum, *Louder Than Words*]

The most striking aspect of the song is a spoken word monologue
(the first on a U2 album). Bono tells of a figure approaching him. With
a rose-red face strewn with shades of a royal flush, this lyricism evokes
imagery of a deck of cards suggesting that this approaching figure is the
dealer for a deadly game in which Bono has no control of the outcome.
He watches this figure slap down hundred-dollar bills representing
the wealth and prosperity that is absent among the village denizens.
Whether the bills are on a table or in Bono's hands is unknown. The
lack of detail about Bono's role, as either an active agent or merely an
observer, adds a level of complexity to the song's narrative as Bono's
character knows that what he is seeing is abhorrent but struggles with
what to do about the figure. Bono's role is fluid as he fluctuates among
anger, hatred, disbelief, and anguish. He is apprehensive at first but then
follows the figure through mud huts and streets. They enter a building
and ascend to the next floor. The figure breathes into a saxophone,
playing notes, just as the sounds of women and children groaning echo
through the walls; a hellish jazz symphonic of greed and devastation.

In *Into the Heart*, Niall Stokes discusses the saxophone imagery,
suggesting the song contrasts the violence with "the liberating sound
of John Coltrane's saxophone breathing" and signifies that America is a
"land of paradoxes." [Stokes, *Into the Heart*, 68] This concept is actual-
ized by Bono repeating the phrase "outside is America," which sounds
as if Bono's character passes from incredulousness to acceptance to fury
at the situation around him. Despite his pacifism and practicing of
nonviolence, Bono had a visceral reaction to what he was seeing during
his travels through Central America. [Rock Hall and Newseum, *Louder*

Than Words] This analysis of America being a land of paradoxes fits into the album's theme regarding its inherent dichotomy.

Because "Bullet the Blue Sky" was written to accuse America of hypocrisy for its involvement in El Salvador, it can be inferred that the figure Bono follows in the monologue is Reagan. The image of Reagan, a white symbol of oppression, and him playing the saxophone, a Black symbol of expression, is infested with hypocrisies. The president's embracing of an art form pioneered by Black Americans such as Coltrane symbolizes the differences between Reagan's approach to foreign and domestic policies. With this imagery, Reagan is mocking the fight for civil rights in El Salvador by flaunting the liberation a movement achieved in America two decades previously.

Following the first segment of Bono's monologue, the violent passion in this scene comes into full effect as the Edge's heavy guitar launches into a solo inspired by Jimi Hendrix, an artist whose virtuosic skills have since been leveraged as the soundtrack to the countercultural protests against America's involvement in the Vietnam War. Although the role of the guitar was minimalized to provide just enough atmospheric context to the song's narrative at the beginning, the Edge now brings the instrument front and center to signify that the war is now here. Outside is America.

Mirroring the increased intensity of the Edge's guitar, Larry and Adam add rhythm textures to the moment. Adam's bass line remains consistent throughout the entire song with a repeating pattern plucked in Em and D, but is mixed with more emphasis during the solo. On the drums, Larry increases the tempo of the bass drum and the sound is mixed in a way to refocus the song's sonic qualities. These contributions from the rhythm section, aided by the production, add depth and nuance to the scene. If the Edge's guitar solo signified the war had reached the village, the rhythm is a soldier pounding on a door.

The Edge's guitar fades into distortion and feedback in the last 20 seconds of the song as Bono recites the second part of his monologue. In just a few lines, he sketches the aftermath of the devastation: rain is pouring through a gaping wound in the sky and pelting women and children. In the final line of the song, Bono recites that they "run into the arms of America." These are the same arms that abetted the violence the villagers endured, rendering the line an indictment of American policy. Even the imagery of marching soldiers and gunfire is washed away in the rain as Adam and Larry end the rhythm section just before Bono recites the last line signifying that the military forces have moved onto the next village to wreak their havoc.

In *U2: Rock 'n' Roll to Change the World*, Neufeld details those ideals of Reagan's that clashed with U2's. He writes that Reagan "championed an aggressive brand of neoconservatism, promoting a strong military buildup, a provocative foreign policy, and a hard-hitting approach to Communism." [Neufeld, *U2*, 52] He notes that this reinvigorated conservatism resulted in tax schemes and deregulation that broadened the wealth gap between the rich and poor. The figure slapping down dollar bills was Reagan financing a violent regime to suit his foreign policy and reinforce what neoconservatives and fundamentalist Christians believed to be righteous to make themselves wealthier, exploiting human beings abroad to convey a misleading sense of prosperity, safety, and security to Americans domestically.

Reagan as the figure in "Bullet the Blue Sky" adds to the significance of the mural Bono saw illustrated in the church. The Pharaoh of the Oppression enslaved the Israelites, while the Pharaoh of the Exodus reigned when Moses led the Israelites in their escape out of Egypt. According to the biblical story, the Pharaoh's heart was hardened by God as he pursued the Israelites. Moses then parted the Red Sea to allow the Israelites to cross and crashed the waters on Pharaoh and his army. The mural symbolized the Salvadorans as the Israelites escaping from the tyranny of America.

Despite the mural, Bono writes about the Salvadoran women and children running into America's arms. There is some thematic confusion with this detail. Certainly, it cannot be the Salvadorans who are running into America's arms as evidenced by the mural. This line would be more fitting to describe Americans seeing Reagan as a figure of salvation as observed by the Edge regarding their unwavering support. This conflation of imagery and ideas could suggest that, although the song was inspired by atrocities in El Salvador, the scene of the damaged village could also represent poverty-stricken and marginalized Americans negatively impacted by Reagan's neoconservative policies. The type of suffering may be different, but everyone outside of Reagan's group of elites is affected. Thus, in alignment with the idea of America being a land of paradoxes, the promise of prosperity and security that Reagan and his fundamentalist Christian supporters championed is an empty one.

Believing that Americans are a generally receptive type of people, Bono also believes it is this inherent quality that allows people to have confidence in dangerous figures like Reagan. Bono suggests that many Americans chose not to see the inherent evil and hypocrisy of Reagan and his political funders because they wanted to believe Reagan would lead a cavalry to rescue them from the economic stagnation and governmental failure of US policies in the 1970s under president Jimmy Carter. Pushing back against the fictional representation of America they had seen on television and in films growing up, Bono asserts that Reagan was just an actor and did not represent ideals based in reality. "It was only a movie," says Bono. "I think the picture's ended now and Americans are leaving the cinema a little down in the mouth." [Stokes, "The World About Us"]

Up to this point, no song in U2's catalog was as acrimonious to injustice on a global scale as "Bullet the Blue Sky." It quickly became a staple in their live performances, appearing in almost every set since. Though the song's origin stemmed from a specific conflict, the overall mood and condemnation against hypocrisy and injustice was later applied to a variety of different scenarios that helped to maintain the song's relevancy over time.

John Jobling illustrates the narrative evolution of "Bullet the Blue Sky" in a live setting in *U2: The Definitive Biography*. During the European shows of the Zoo TV tour in the early 1990s, Jobling says that the video screens displayed "flaming crosses morphed into swastikas . . . warning of the similarities between Europe's present state and that of the '30s" with the stars of the European Union flag tumbling down and juxtaposing it with clips of Nazi propaganda such as Leni Riefenstahl's *Triumph of the Will*. [Jobling, *U2*, 232] Following the September 11th attacks and US thirst for revenge, Jobling cites blogger Chris Conroy who said the song "became a disturbing experience" with the audience "losing themselves in the brutality of the music and not in the lyrics of condemnation for the exercise of force." [Jobling, *U2*, 288] The fear of violent retribution against a group of people, specifically people of color, likely resulted in U2 changing their approach with the song to a pragmatic one and visually channeling the audience's and band's aggression to faceless ideas such as Wall Street and capitalism, including featuring footage of police in riot gear battling with protestors, as seen in the Innocence + Experience tour in 2015.

For The Joshua Tree Tour 2017, the narrative of "Bullet the Blue Sky" broadened to condemn Trump because his policies had a potentially more devastating reach than previous conflicts the song was adapted to address. To promote the tour, U2 performed the song on *The Tonight Show with Jimmy Fallon* but changed some of the lyrics to address Trump using Twitter to provoke North Korea into nuclear con-

flict. Bono substituted Reagan for Trump in the song's signature monologue with "suit and tie comes up to me" and that the figure had "skin
as thin as orange crush," which was a dig at Trump's appearance. Even
like Reagan in the original, Trump slaps hundred-dollar bills down.
The monologue in the performance continues, citing weeping children
"vaporized in a single tweet" and Americans feeling alone despite the
illuminated lights of the president's home. The president is there, but he
is not leading. [Fallon, interview]

In an interview with *Rolling Stone*, Bono expressed the vulnerability
of US democracy that Trump exposed and exploited. Trump's fanatical
nationalism was a stark reminder that America's self-awareness and
identity did not evolve on their own. Although U2 have always strived
to apply partisanship to their approach to activism and worked across
both sides of the political aisle, they recognized an existential threat
in Trump. For Bono, democracy requires a lot of attention to keep it
safeguarded from ideological forces that aim to destroy it. [Greene,
"Bono on How"] Though *The Joshua Tree* and its 30th anniversary tour
addressed this threat, it is the intensity and cathartic energy of "Bullet
the Blue Sky" that makes our collective outrage valid and it the most
politically relevant song on the album.

Throughout Trump's term as president, America witnessed new
extremes in the neoconservative ideals Reagan championed throughout
the 1980s. Although Reagan's aggressive approach to governing was
shaped and driven by Christian fundamentalism, Trump's adaptation of
his "Let's Make America Great Again" slogan had evolved to energize
and embolden the white supremacist faction not only within the Christian fundamentalist movement but also those outside of it as well. Con-
flating the two movements, Trump had emboldened a white nationalist
movement that demanded a more refined and enhanced version of the
ideals Reagan advocated for during his presidency, policies and actions
that represented an uncompromising and strong-willed approach

against any foreign or leftist influence that is perceived to threaten the wealth and safety of any group of Americans Trump, his administration, and his most staunch supporters believed to be legitimate. Within the Trump administration, these alleged threats included non-white and non-Christian Americans both natural-born and naturalized, as well as immigrants and refugees.

Although "Bullet the Blue Sky" was initially written to condemn a nationalist movement built on military strength promoted by Reagan to rationalize his foreign policy, the song remains relevant as Trump empowered clandestine white power nationalism to rationalize his domestic policy. Bono's lyrics condemning foreign intervention in Central America orchestrated by a saxophone-playing Reagan easily translates to Trump. Trump simultaneously declared that his administration did more to benefit Black Americans than any other president, while at the same time denouncing racial justice groups such as Black Lives Matter because of their criticism of his administration's policies and the negative effects many of his extremist supporters inflicted on racial justice advocacy efforts. Trump's appropriation and dismissal of the mission and focus of racial justice groups and protests were designed to fuel the animosity of his white nationalist and supremacist base and encourage them to identify their opposition as threats against American security and prosperity. Within this modern context, Trump embodied the saxophone-blowing figure that approaches Bono during the song's monologue, exploiting racial justice grassroots efforts to incite white nationalist and supremacist violence to maintain power as a president focused on establishing and maintaining law and order—a dog whistle to these extremist nationalist and white supremacist supporters seeking to shape America to reflect their own racist beliefs.

U2's admiration of Dr. King's teachings regarding those who repeat history when they fail to remember the past ring true when considering the relevancy of "Bullet the Blue Sky" within the Trump era. Much like the song's original intent of highlighting the hypocrisies of Reagan exploiting a civil rights movement in El Salvador to champion fundamentalist policies despite America's own history, "Bullet the Blue Sky" also reveals the Trump administration's own hypocrisy. U2 recognized this three decades after recording *The Joshua Tree* when commenting on the danger Trump's presidency posed to the freedoms of all Americans beyond his most ardent white supremacist supporters. While Reagan exploited Central Americans to elevate the wealth and prosperity of Christian fundamentalists, Trump exploited the United States' original sin of racism to advance his own well-being. The only difference is that instead of the jungles of Central America, Trump brought the bloodshed home.

CHAPTER FOUR

Hear Their Heartbeat

A DECADE BEFORE U2 TOOK TO THE STAGE TO CONDEMN THE US government for its role in atrocities across Central America, an unspeakable horror was taking place in South America. Fearing for their lives, many citizens remained silent about crimes committed against their communities by the military juntas and coups that overthrew their democratically elected governments. Something had to be done to show courage in the face of their oppressors. Before Bono championed justice against the violence he witnessed, a group of people stood up and spoke out: women.

U2 were in the middle of recording *The Joshua Tree* when they interrupted the sessions to perform as part of A Conspiracy of Hope, a series of six benefit concerts supporting Amnesty International in June 1986. After the band's first performance on the tour in Daly City, a city along the southern edge of San Francisco, California, Bono met a Chilean mural artist named René Castro. According to *The Heart of the Mission: Latino Art and Politics in San Francisco* by Cary Cordova, Castro was one of four Chilean artists whose group was referred to as the Brigada Orlando Letelier. Named after the Chilean diplomat Orlando Letelier who, in 1976, was assassinated in a car bombing in Washington, DC, orchestrated by agents of Chile's secret police called Dirección de

Inteligencia Nacional, this collective consisted of Castro, Beyhan Cagri, and Letelier's two sons, Francisco and José, as they painted murals that "resembled the 'flat style' of murals that decorated Chile during the Salvador Allende government, which the Pinochet government sought to eradicate." [Cordova, *The Heart of the Mission*, 175]

Through his artwork, Castro was an ardent critic of Augusto Pinochet who, in 1973, led a coup d'état, supported by the United States as part of a larger campaign of political repression and state terror across South America called Operation Condor, against the democratically elected socialist president Salvador Allende before consolidating power, ending civilian rule, and assuming the role of president of Chile. In his home country, Castro actively protested the Pinochet regime through his artwork, which resulted in him being detained and tortured in a Chilean concentration camp for two years before being exiled. Bono and Castro met after Bono visited San Francisco's Balmy Alley in the Mission District to view Castro's larger mural works. Bono was fascinated by Castro's story and the message inherent in his work. In an interview in May 1987, Bono said that he developed an interest in Central America after meeting Castro. Their friendship developed when Castro discovered Bono's connection to Amnesty International, the human rights organization that Castro believed had come to his aid and saved him. Castro had been imprisoned following Allende's death and was tortured, including having a hole bored through his chest. Before being rescued by Amnesty International, Castro was also held in the same stadium were Victor Jara, the Chilean singer and activist, was killed. As their connection strengthened, which included Castro giving Bono some of his paintings, he was eventually asked to go to Central America. [Irwin, "This Is What We Do Best"]

Though Chilean, Castro's mural work was a rallying cry to criticize the injustices permeating throughout Central and South America. According to Cordova, the liberation of these people "spoke to the dreams of thousands of people in the United States," including the art- ists of the Brigada Orlando Letelier who had personally been victims of violence perpetrated by their homeland's governments. [Cordova, *The Heart of the Mission*, 174] For Castro, painting these murals meant taking "risks going to zones where people are oppressed and abused" and denouncing the violence in his work.

During the A Conspiracy of Hope concerts, Bono learned about the source of oppression and violence Castro protested against and became aware of an organization called the Madres de Plaza de Mayo (Mothers of the Plaza de Mayo). The Madres de Plaza de Mayo consists of Argentine mothers whose children were secretly abducted by their government between 1976 and 1983. Known as being "disappeared," these forceful kidnappings were carried against students and dissi- dents who were critical of the Argentinian military junta that carried out a coup in 1976 that was also supported by the United States. The Madres de Plaza de Mayo were the first organization to protest the human rights issue of forceful disappearances when they marched in 1977 wearing white head scarves to protest and raise awareness of the crimes, campaign for transparency within the Argentine government, and demand information pertaining to the location of the bodies and the circumstances behind their deaths.

While on his mission through El Salvador, Bono met representa- tives of a similar organization called the Comité de Madres Monsignor Romero (CoMadres: Committee of the Mothers Monsignor Romero), which consisted of mothers protesting the disappearing of children and relatives during the Salvadoran civil war. Through his humanitarian work at this time, Bono came to fully understand the mission these women were on because he witnessed atrocities firsthand. "People would just disappear," Bono said after recalling seeing a body thrown from a van. "If you were part of the opposition, you might find an SUV with the windows blacked out parked outside your house. If that didn't stop you, occasionally they would come in and take you and murder you; there would be no trial." [McCormick and U2, *U2 by U2*, 184]

In *U2: The Definitive Biography*, John Jobling profiles an account from David Batstone, founder of the Central American Mission Partners (CAMP), of Bono and Ali spending an afternoon with some mothers from CoMadres in their office in San Salvador. "I still remember he and Ali being brought to tears," says Batstone, "by these mothers whose kids had disappeared and were never seen again and the work that they were doing in El Salvador to keep the profile of their sons and daughters alive. That was a very moving experience for them." [Jobling, *U2*, 159] Bono, in conversation with music journalist Michka Assayas, reflected on the experience as well by saying,

> These women who had their children abducted and murdered by the secret police didn't even know where they had been buried. They had no place, no graveyard to mourn. These women, these mothers, their stories, I will remember, always. [Assayas, *Bono*, 208]

This was during the same trip to El Salvador that inspired Bono to write and U2 to record "Bullet the Blue Sky." Although "Bullet the Blue Sky" was laced with violent fury and condemnation aimed at Reagan's military intervention in the region, the experience meeting with members of CoMadres, coupled with the stories of the Madres de Plaza de Mayo and mothers from elsewhere in Central and South America, inspired Bono to write a solemn hymn lamenting these mothers and their pain. The song, "Mothers of the Disappeared," according to Carter Alan in *Outside Is America*, points "an accusing finger at America's foreign policy, which supported some of the violently repressive governments responsible for the killings." [Alan, *Outside Is America*, 151]

Forgoing the use of biblical imagery as he did with "Bullet the Blue Sky" to condemn US intervention and foreign policy, for "Mothers of the Disappeared" Bono is unambiguous and explicit with the song's message. The sons and daughters, Bono sings in the opening lines from the perspective of one of the mothers, had their lives cut down when stolen away by their oppressive government. He conveys the pain these mothers feel as they are continuously haunted by the memories of their children, their children's laughter heard in the wind with the rain signifying tears.

The pain and anguish these mothers feel is illustrated in the lines about the night coming down like a hanged prisoner in shades of black and blue, connecting the imagery to a bruised and beaten body. These lines thematically provide insight into the experience of these mothers. In many cases, the disappearances of their children and relatives occurred at night or that is when they were executed or murdered. Nighttime descends on the mothers because they feel helpless and confused, unable to find any clue as to where their children are. The absence of light in the scene is driven by the lack of government transparency regarding what happened to the victims, black and blue from beatings and camouflaged by the darkness. This imprisonment of nightfall symbolizes a mother's internal grief as well as an external struggle as, over four decades later, many of these women still search for answers and still hold protests and demonstrations to raise awareness and demand justice. The night is a constant reminder of their agony, which surrounds them with helplessness and confusion as they remain the victims of a deadly power struggle with an oppressive regime to obtain closure.

In the final verse, the connection the mothers have to their children is conveyed with heart-wrenching imagery. Bono sings that the sons stand naked in the trees and the cries of the daughters can be heard through the walls, evoking imagery of hangings and rape, respectively. Haunted by their pain, the mothers conceive their children's suffering. Though they do not have a clear and definitive understanding of what happened to their children, the mothers envision the pain and torment.

Not only do the missed opportunities and little moments of everyday life tear open their wounds and prevent them from completely healing, but they are also haunted by visions of their children in the midst of their demise and forced to play out the horror over and over again.

Bono's experience in Central America left an incredible impression on him that resulted in two of *The Joshua Tree*'s most emotionally driven tracks. The severe reaction of "Bullet the Blue Sky" is counterbalanced by the bereavement of "Mothers of the Disappeared," which serves to be another way to process pain from similar situations. "Bullet the Blue Sky" results in Bono reacting violently, whereas in *Into the Heart*, Stokes claims the latter song is "an act of witness" with "no optimistic note of reassurance." [Stokes, *Into the Heart*, 77] Although Stokes is correct that the song witnesses the grief of these mothers and a lack of reassurance in the form of closure, I disagree with the notion that there is absolutely no optimism in the song. "Mothers of the Disappeared" is a dark, emotional manifestation of unimaginable suffering, but U2 finds slivers of hope in even the most desperate and devastating of circumstances.

Despite much of the grim imagery and narrative within "Mothers of the Disappeared," there is indeed an enduring sense of hope. Throughout the song, Bono repeats the line "hear their heartbeat" and the significance of this line is multifaceted. In one aspect, hearing the heartbeat of their children represents a maternal closeness that cannot be quashed, and that despite seeing their tears and hearing their cries, the heartbeat is indicative of a spirit within the mother that no government or military junta can take away. It is the hope for the mother and child reunion and the eternal bond between them. That heartbeat was formed in the womb and, even after birth and their children's death, the emotional and physical connection remains unbroken. "Hear their heartbeat" is a subtle, yet powerful, detail about the strength of a mother's love and the struggle it can overcome. In the same vein, it can also be a catalyst for extreme suffering. Hearing the heartbeats of their children while having no clarity as to their whereabouts keeps both the memory of their children and their sustained grief alive.

The heartbeat imagery in the song could also represent the ongoing advocacy of CoMadres and the Madres de Plaza de Mayo and their defiance against the silence of their respective government's involvement in the disappearances of their children. Still, nearly five decades later, these mothers are committed to finding the whereabouts of their stolen children even as they become older, with ancillary organizations forming such as the Asociación Civil Abuelas de Plaza de Mayo (The Grandmothers of the Plaza de Mayo). These mothers in their ongoing defense of human rights are galvanized by the heartbeats of their children and the hope that someday they will find answers. When Bono sings about hearing the heartbeats, it speaks to what both devastates and drives these women to stand up to their oppressors. Even in death, the spirit of their children drives these mothers to make their countries and, by extension, the world a better place for all women and their children. The power behind the line "hear their heartbeat" comes from the duality of its meaning: a lamentation and a call to action. The song, acting as a prayer, serves a need to seek clarity in the present and guidance to prevent this from happening again.

Stokes frames his comment about the lack of optimism in "Mothers of the Disappeared" by noting the track was chosen to close the album. Through *The Joshua Tree*, until the final track, the listener has journeyed with U2 as the band came to understand the dichotomy of America as well as their own Irishness in relation. During that journey, there has been celebration and tears, representing the fractured joy and unforgiving cruelty of a hypocritical America. Stokes rationalizes his assertion regarding the absence of optimism in "Mothers of the Disappeared" by suggesting that Bono concedes the world contains too much evil that cannot always be explained or understood. [Stokes, *Into the Heart*, 77] Although there is much evil in this world, I do not conflate that concept with the rationale of closing the album with this particular song. If the overall theme of *The Joshua Tree*, and its exploration of an America with many different faces, is to highlight that America can rise above its own hypocrisy and be a promised land, ending the album with a message of hopelessness and defeat does not contribute to that narrative. America's actions and policies have indeed caused pain to people both within and beyond its borders, but it is not powerful enough as to completely destroy the human spirit.

Although the lyrics of "Mothers of the Disappeared" depict the misery these mothers endure, the emotional power of Bono telling their story comes from his vocal delivery. At the beginning, he sings quietly but barely more audible than a whisper. At this stage in the song, he sounds as if he is praying but with a tinge of intense energy brewing beneath the surface. The listener has experienced the extent of Bono's violent declaration within "Bullet the Blue Sky," but in "Mothers of the Disappeared," there is an internal struggle. There is a desire for a strong reaction toward the atrocities these mothers have experienced, but Bono is too overwhelmed by his anger. As the song progresses, the drama of this vocal delivery is heightened as Bono emotes and expresses more anguish with each passing verse. He is on the verge of breaking through that emotional barrier and striking down evil with a vengeance, but the pain he channels is far too great for such senselessness. Such an "eye for an eye" vengeance is beneath the dignity of the mothers whose pain he is conveying.

The emotional breakdown at the end of the final verse results in the most dynamic and thematically moving quality of the song. At 3:37, two simultaneous vocal tracks begin to counterplay each other in Bono's struggle with the range of the pain he is channeling: one being a muted sorrowful moaning with the other being a falsetto wail of anguish. "The keening that [Bono] does in that is kind of prehistoric," said Adam, "it connects with something very primitive." [McCormick and U2, *U2 by U2*, 184]

In his essay "Vocal Layering as Deconstruction and Reinvention in U2" in the collection *Exploring U2*, Christopher Endrinal documents various examples of U2's use of vocal layering and multitracking within their songs, which Endrinal calls "multiregister layering," to describe the band's process of recording several versions of the same vocal line but in different registers. The purpose of this process is to use Bono's wide vocal range to create a dynamic mood with each vocal track playing against the other to create a thematic atmosphere that adds to the track's narrative. [Endrinal, "Vocal Layering," 69] There is conflict within Bono as he struggles to express himself within "Mothers of the Disappeared." While the muted moaning is the most obvious vocal line in this part of the track, the falsetto wail is buried in the back of the production, barely audible but still present as if to suggest Bono's urge to be angry is still there even if he cannot express that outright. Perhaps what Bono acknowledges is that sometimes one can be too exhausted and drained to be enraged, making way for grief to take over.

"Mothers of the Disappeared" is the prayer for the women and children victimized by Reagan's foreign policy that closes out *The Joshua Tree*. "There is no question in my mind that the people of America, through their taxes, are paying for the equipment that is used to torture people in El Salvador" said Bono. [*Propaganda*, "The Enduring Chill"] After the explosive fury of "Bullet the Blue Sky," U2's goal was to musically channel the story of these mothers in a somber way that accentuated the spirituality behind their pain. Creating music that served as a hymn to support the prayer the lyrics embodied was key to adding dignity to the song.

Closing out *The Joshua Tree*, "Mothers of the Disappeared" was, due to contributions from Brian Eno on the production, the most experimental track on the album. Although many of the album's other tracks were entrenched in or contained elements of American roots music, "Mothers of the Disappeared" exhibited none of the qualities from those songs. In the *Classic Albums* documentary, Adam described Eno's contributions as adding a darkened sound evoking a death squad. [*Classic Albums, The Joshua Tree*]

Eno was essential in giving the song the darkness it needed to convey the seriousness of the narrative. Opening the song are Eno's synthesizer and keyboards, creating an effect with the sound reminiscent of light rain hitting a village roof but processed with an electronic quality that is splintering and unnerving, like the icy presence of death creeping in. Coming in after 50 seconds is Adam's bass and a processed drum loop from Larry, produced by Eno and mixed by Lanois, which results in a droning and synthesized quality that Adam described as "so eerie and foreign and scary." [McCormick and U2, *U2 by U2*, 184] In an article for *The Joshua Tree*'s 20th anniversary, Colm O'Hare of *Hot Press* discusses Eno's processing of Larry's drum loop and the drone texture it created as being "the key sonic element" of the song which created an atmosphere with "an abstract sense of evil and dread." [O'Hare, "The Secret History"]

Along with Adam and Larry, the Edge comes in with his guitar playing a melody written by Bono on a Spanish guitar. Adam recalled that the melody for "Mothers of the Disappeared" came from the melody of a song Bono used to sing to Ethiopian children about basic hygiene practices. [McCormick and U2, *U2 by U2*, 184] The repurposing of this melody is interesting considering the melody's origin and inclusion on *The Joshua Tree* pertaining to children, albeit over different issues. This direction might not be unheard of for U2 as, noted by Stokes in *Into the Heart*, the band is likely continuing a tradition of closing out their albums with songs musically resembling lullabies, like "40" on *War* or "MLK" on *The Unforgettable Fire*, but the devastating subject matter of "Mothers of the Disappeared" makes it more of a lament than the closing tracks on those two albums. [Stokes, *Into the Heart*, 77]

While touring for *The Joshua Tree* in 1987, "Mothers of the Disappeared" was performed only seven times. Perhaps the biggest reason for this is, according to Bryan Wawzenek of *Diffuser*, that "the austere and experimental qualities of the song made it a tune that wasn't the easiest to perform in concert." [Wawzenek, "Mothers of the Disappeared"] Given the experimental attributes developed by Eno for the song, that may have been true. It also speaks to the other likely reason being the song's troubling subject matter and U2's criticism of the Reagan administration and the role America played supporting the repression and terror of right-wing dictatorships across Central and South America that resulted in the human rights abuses that inspired the song. Though "Bullet the Blue Sky" was also critical of the Reagan administration for its intervention in Central America, the message may have been misunderstood by some concertgoers amid the poetic biblical imagery, the band's aggressive energy during the performance, and the shifting focus of the song's narrative within a live setting since 1987. This could possibly explain why, after the band last performed "Mothers of the Disappeared" at Sun Devil Stadium in Tempe, Arizona, on December 20, 1987 (filmed for, but not included in, the 1988 music documentary *Rattle and Hum*), the song would not be performed in America again until they performed it on May 14, 2017, in Seattle, Washington, for *The Joshua Tree*'s 30th anniversary.

However, "Mothers of the Disappeared" would be performed solely by Bono and the Edge since its return during a concert in Buenos Aires, Argentina, on February 5, 1998, more than a decade after it was last performed. In the country where the government disappeared dissidents nearly three decades previously, the performance of the song was an opportunity to condemn the Argentine government and make a statement about the human rights abuses they carried out. During the performance of "Mothers of the Disappeared," members of the Madres de Plaza de Mayo accompanied the band on stage.

In a concert in Chile on February 11, 1998, U2 would play footage of the Madres on the stage's projection screen and again were joined on stage by mothers whose children were forcibly disappeared. The concert was performed at the Estadio Nacional in Santiago, which had formerly held a prison camp during Pinochet's regime, and was broadcasted live on Chilean television. In conversation with Michka Assayas, Bono reflected on that performance with the mothers saying:

> We asked for the show to be televised that night. Most of the population couldn't afford tickets and be able to see it. I brought the *madres* out on to the stage, and they said the name of the missing children into the microphone. Then I spoke to Pinochet as if he was there, as if he was watching television, which I'm sure he wasn't. I just said: "Mister Pinochet, God will be your judge, but at the very least, tell these women where the bones of their children are buried, because years later they still don't know where their loved ones are." [Assayas, *Bono*, 307]

The Joshua Tree Tour 2017 was the first time since the Tempe concert in 1987 that "Mothers of the Disappeared" was performed by the entire band. Although Chilean and Argentine mothers were not brought out onto the stage like they were two decades previously, the concert's video projections during the performance depicted faceless mothers walking slowly out of a shadowy mist toward the audience and holding candles. The mothers are still looking for answers while their stories are being told so many years later.

"Mothers of the Disappeared" makes for the most fitting song to end *The Joshua Tree* on multiple levels. The lyrics are the most direct and unambiguous of any song on the rest of the album with a narrative that is universally understood in its impact and breadth. The experimentation, aided by Eno's production and synthesizer as well as Lanois' mixing, indicated that the band were in the early stages of breaking new musical ground within the group. Bono's vocal delivery signified his exhaustion with the extent of the destructive influence of America. All of these things, when combined together, create a sense that U2 had, on *The Joshua Tree*, unconsciously reached the end of their American journey. Although it would take a few more years for the band to fully realize this and change their physical and musical aesthetic in the early 1990s with the release of *Achtung Baby*, the painful lament of "Mothers of the Disappeared" is the logical end point of the story. Sometimes there are no answers, only a need to learn from the past to try to influence the future.

The relevancy of "Mothers of the Disappeared" can be recontextualized when considering the immigration enforcement policy Trump's administration enacted in 2018. In May, the US Department of Justice enacted broad measures to detain migrants who unlawfully crossed the border between the United States and Mexico. Aligned with Trump's America First vision when guiding foreign and domestic policies, Trump's administration enforced policies to separate migrant children from their mothers. As these migrant mothers were detained awaiting updates regarding their asylum status, they were unaware of the location of their children and the condition of their health and safety.

Trump's stringent immigration policies, driven by a white nationalist agenda, were not far removed from the forced disappearances of children in Central and South America given his administration's failure to properly document and reunite many migrant families crossing the border. Thousands of families were separated, with parents and children detained in overcrowded and underserved facilities far away from each other, and many migrants died while detained or in custody by US Immigration and Customs Enforcement (ICE). Although it can be argued these measures are not nearly as brutal as those enacted by the regimes in Central and South America during the 1970s and 1980s, the motivation behind them is still cruel and the system's inherent failures a reflection of that. The US Department of Health and Human Services, in a report issued in September 2019, cited that migrant children exhibited feelings of extreme abandonment and post-traumatic stress. In 2020, the Southern Poverty Law Center sued the Trump administration for its egregious cruelty of separating migrant families.

The ongoing practice of separating mothers from their children, either through murderous foreign regimes or its own government bureaucratic immigration process, clashes with the perceptions of those who have come to seek refuge within US borders. U2 because of their Irishness, like generations before them, had a deep spiritual connection with America as a refuge where one can seek security and opportunity, which are things that asylum seekers also desire. However, such perceptions were illusory especially as Trump alienated America from the rest of the world. "Mothers of the Disappeared," in a modern context, represents U2 expressing an ongoing call to action for governments to cease ripping children away from their mothers because the song emphasizes that a mother's deeply rooted primal grief knows no borders.

CHAPTER FIVE

Deeper into Black

U2'S EXISTENTIAL JOURNEY THROUGH AMERICA, IN LARGE PART, HAD them looking outwardly to understand the vastness and extent of America's flaws. As outsiders, they could observe and rebuke the country's failures at the hands of ignorance or indifference. While they explored the dark reality of America's dichotomy, exposing themselves to that darkness revealed something sinister within them. Toward the end of their journey recording *The Joshua Tree*, U2 would learn that admonishing the things around you meant bringing down one's own guard and confronting the darkness within.

While U2 had explored America's western landscape and drew inspiration from the beauty and starkness of its deserts, Bono also spent time reading works from quintessential American heartland authors who explored the darker aspects of American life on the brink of oblivion and humanity. Bono recalled these works in *U2 by U2* saying that he was inspired to write a song exploring the demented mind of a murderer after reading books such as Norman Mailer's *The Executioner's Song* and Truman Capote's *In Cold Blood*. For Bono, crafting a narrative exploring the inner darkness of a deranged lunatic was a means of grasping and reconciling his own inner darkness, one he believes exists in everyone. "Violence is something I know quite a bit about," said

Bono. "I have a side of me which, in a corner, can be very violent. It's the least attractive thing in anyone and I wanted to own up to that." [McCormick and U2, *U2 by U2*, 184]

Influenced by the American literature he was reading by authors such as Mailer and Capote, as well as Flannery O'Connor and Raymond Carver, Bono became fascinated with the inner workings of a killer's mind. By exploring what people think when they make the irreversible decision to take a life, Bono could juxtapose those feelings of power and dominance with his own internal demons. U2 had observed and experienced so much of what America offered, both in terms of foreign policy and its own domestic issues, that there became an inherent need to purge a demon from within themselves if they were going to end their American journey mentally and spiritually intact. Exorcising a demon they had lived with while recording *The Joshua Tree* became a means of survival.

The song's narrative origins were inspired by the celebrity of American heartland murders that occurred during the middle of the twentieth century. In addition to the media circus that would surround these murders, their stories would then be romanticized in novels as part of a literary movement called "new journalism," which combined journalistic reporting with fiction writing. While Bono was crafting his portrait of a deranged mind, two criminal cases stood out particularly for their extreme brutishness in terms of the heinous acts committed and the sensationalist responses by the US media and justice system that followed.

In 1976, Gary Gilmore shot and murdered two people in Utah, a gas station attendant named Max Jensen and a motel manager named Ben Bushnell, during two separate instances during the course of two days. Gilmore was only tried for Bushnell's murder, since Jensen's had no witnesses, and was sentenced to death on October 7, 1976, after the US Supreme Court restored capital punishment in July of that year. Gilmore then unintentionally became the center of a national debate about the ethics of the death penalty, which earned him some celebrity status. Despite Gilmore's statements and actions about his desire to die, which manifested in a hunger strike and two suicide attempts, he was used as a prop to debate the constitutionality of the death penalty. Gilmore would eventually be put to death in January 1977 after choosing the unorthodox, and quite archaic, execution of death by firing squad. Gilmore's case was the inspiration for Mailer's *The Executioner's Song*.

The other case, which was the basis for Capote's *In Cold Blood*, was inspired by the 1959 murders of a Kansas family by two drifters, Richard Hickock and Perry Edward Smith. Smith and Hickock robbed, and eventually murdered, the members of the Clutter family in their home. Both murderers went to trial and were sentenced to death for their crimes. Whereas Mailer had written his book based on interviews with the families of Gilmore's and his victims, Capote actually interviewed the killers for *In Cold Blood* as part of his examination of the deceit of a bucolic America in the 1950s while attempting to analyze and reconstruct the conditions in which one makes the conscious decision to commit a murder. Following in the path of these nonfiction novelists, Bono would craft his own new journalist take on those who live, whether by choice, on the fringes of the American Dream.

"Exit," the penultimate track on *The Joshua Tree*, became that exploration of a deranged mind living as an outcast of the American Dream. With the opening lines, warning that the subject of the narrative has a mind that has gone astray with their alleged cure suggesting malevolent intent, the introduction of Bono's story immediately makes it clear that this killer is making a conscious decision. That, unlike many Americans who are unable to achieve the American Dream even if they wanted to, this dark figure at the heart of "Exit" is seeking his own demise by exploiting the flawed construct of the American Dream.

Continuing the first verse, the figure stays awake so as not to dream. Early on, the song takes a narratively complex approach as the listener has to figure out the context and meaning of these dreams that drives the figure's psychosis. The figure is fighting against a darkness in his dreams that urges him to carry out his primal murderous impulses, an inherent sickness, and staying awake keeps him from mentally and emotionally crossing that threshold. Not dreaming becomes an act of avoidance or perhaps resignation, a refusal to play into the illusion of the American Dream just as much as a response to the nightmares the American Dream fuels in his mind. With this, the subject of "Exit" is reconciling some internal struggle and his own desperate circumstances.

At the end of the first verse, Bono sings that the figure wanted to believe in the hands of love. He wants to believe that love is a salvation, but for some reason he acts against it. Whether this comes from a realization that his yearning for love is impossible, due to it either being denied to him or that he was incapable of experiencing it, something has gone wrong and the subject feels compelled to react. Regarding love and the American Dream, or a conflation of the two, the figure's reaction is a response to his desire for something he neither has nor can believe in, a perverted manifestation of both concepts that he feels have failed him.

In a concert at the Los Angeles Memorial Coliseum in 1987, Bono told the audience that "Exit" was a song about a religious man who had become extremely dangerous because he could not decipher the enigmatic riddle of the hands of love, the duality where one could both build and destroy. [Christopher, "Exit"] Religious imagery had been used throughout U2's catalog, and *The Joshua Tree* is no exception. With the album exploring the vastness of America, seeing how the outsiders and outcasts of US society interpreted religion to carry out wickedness was essential in completely understanding the minutiae and extremes of the country's dichotomy. In this case, that dichotomy would include America's endorsement of the role fundamentalist Christianity played into the devastation caused by the country's foreign policy and juxtapose it with the sensationalism that would arise from a lone individual killing in the name of Christianity. One cause was acceptable because of the validation given by the rich hands guiding it while the other being reprehensible, but sparking fascination and sensationalism, in its exploitation of religion.

Following the first verse, the listener follows the mind and footsteps of the killer as he traverses the landscape amid the sounds of dogs crying like men whose hearts have been torn apart by their own inadequacy and failures. In his pocket, the man feels the cold steel of a pistol and fingers the trigger, anticipating the glorious firing of the bullet signifying the release of something deeply rooted within himself. The man is journeying deep into black and white, highlighting the duality of his thoughts and actions: the blackness of his murderous intent against the whiteness of the virtue he feels for carrying it out. Meanwhile, he is conscious of his heart beating, and he feels the misguided roots of his love bursting forth.

The twisted journey of "Exit" comes to a thematic conclusion with the most telling and engaging lines of the song. Closing out the track, Bono declares that the hands of the man in the song are ones capable of both building up and tearing down love, perhaps representative that all human beings' hands are capable of committing acts of terror or adoration. These closing lines reinforce the idea that the killer in the song is making a conscious decision to take someone's life. That narrative seems clear throughout the song. Although, within the construct of achieving or being denied the American Dream, the closing lines are also an indictment of America just as much as declaration from a lone killer.

In the liner notes of a box set commemorating the 20th anniversary of *The Joshua Tree* in 2007, Adam said that the lyrics of "Exit" were written as a commentary regarding the US government's role in international conflicts through military interventions. This analysis certainly echoes what Bono had said in *U2 by U2* about having to confront his own internal demons to adequately understand and address the violence committed through US foreign policy. [McCormick and U2, *U2 by U2*, 184] Although the song's narrative may be about an individual on the surface, the distinction Adam and Bono make about US foreign policy could also suggest that the figure is a manifestation of America itself venturing out into the world to commit atrocities based on its own sense of global superiority just as much as it could be about the type of unstable person who gives in to evil after being left behind by his or her own country. This conflation of ideas gives a fluidity to the concept of the American Dream in "Exit" by portraying a narrative that can either be applied to an individual or collective level.

In an interview conducted by Anna Diamond for *Smithsonian Magazine*, historian Sarah Churchwell, in her book *Behold, America*, discusses the origin of the American Dream and how the concept has been shaped over the 20th century. During the interview, Churchwell says,

> "The American Dream" has always been about the prospect of success, but 100 years ago, the phrase meant the opposite of what it does now. The original "American Dream" was not a dream of individual wealth; it was a dream of equality, justice and democracy for the nation. The phrase was repurposed by each generation, until the Cold War, when it became an argument for a consumer capitalist version of democracy. Our ideas about the "American Dream" froze in the 1950s. Today, it doesn't occur to anybody that it could mean anything else. [Diamond, "American Dream"]

In this, Churchwell is suggesting that the original concept of the American Dream as initially constructed was meant to be, as U2 believed prior to recording *The Joshua Tree*, a dream that all can share. Though, as U2 would find while recording the album, America had failed to live up to the original design of the dream and instead pursued hypocritical foreign policies, broadened the wealth gap, and excluded and alienated minorities and other marginalized groups. The refusal for the country to live up to the ideals of the American Dream as a collective idea fails everyone and motivates those on the fringes to violently retaliate when they feel like they are left behind in a "consumer capitalist version of democracy" and are then individualized as being the exception to the rule—the lone wolf.

In his book, *Walk On: The Spiritual Journey of U2*, Steve Stockman says of "Exit" that "Bono . . . eyeballed the love and goodness of the Christian faith with the demonic, darker side" and that it also "communicated the truth about a disturbing reality . . . about any Christian world-view that would rather sweep that beneath a theological carpet than wrestle with it." [Stockman, *Walk On*, 79] The overall theme of *The Joshua Tree*, including its condemnation of US policies and their destructive effects, illustrates Stockman's assessment. Much like the broader hypocrisy within the country's own inherent dichotomy, so is the US form of extremist Christianity adopted to rationalize cold-blooded murder, with U2 urging Christians and their leaders to resolve these issues through introspection of their beliefs and practices in order to address the unintended consequences.

Though the song does not explicitly indicate that the figure in "Exit" is a man of the cloth, he is modeled after characters from the books Bono was reading at the time like O'Connor's *Wise Blood*, a novel about a discharged serviceman turned nihilist street preacher named Hazel Motes who murders another street preacher for being a false prophet and then blinds himself as an act of atonement. Within the lyrics, the theological beliefs and inclinations are contained within the subject's rationalization that the same hands that can build are also the ones that can destroy. Therein lies the more demonic interpretation of Christianity as the man in "Exit," much like Hazel Motes in O'Connor's novel, kills in accordance to his own devilish brand of Christianity. This realizes the hypocrisy Stockman notes that more mainstream versions of Christianity tend to ignore and is translated into the unwillingness of America to mitigate its own darker elements to narrow its dichotomy.

Up to this point in U2's career, "Exit" was one of the band's darkest songs—not just lyrically in its portrait of the mind of a killer but musically as well. The track was recorded on the last day of *The Joshua Tree* sessions. "Exit" was initially a part of a larger piece stemming from a jam session before being edited down by Eno during the production. [McCormick and U2, *U2 by U2*, 184]

"Exit" opens with Adam's bassline coupled with the sound reminiscent of crickets to add atmospheric tension in a musical landscape where this murderous figure in Bono's lyrics could wander through the night. The Edge's guitar slowly fades in with an effect sounding like a desolate wind but eventually adds character with a needling sound as the strings are played. During this time, the only percussion is an uninterrupted snapping sound. Larry's drums do not come in until well after a minute. These subtle elements mix together to create an anxious setting for the listener. It is not clear as to whether musically we are inside the killer's head or if these are the sounds the victim hears right before being preyed upon. Either way, it is a disturbing ambience that creates a discomfort as the listener is forced to visualize and confront the darkest side of humanity.

Bono's vocals build up from a hushed eeriness increasing in volume and intensity as the song progresses. When singing of a howling wind and the killer's descent into blackness as he holds his weapon of choice, Bono's vocals become a cry for mercy as the killer teeters on the brink of giving into man's most ancient and primeval craving. Bono calls out for his love, perhaps an individual or idea, before the Edge launches into a distorted guitar solo that is gritty in its execution and expression of brutality within the scene as Larry is beating the drums almost murderously. The violent episode is over when the guitar and drums retreat, leaving only a pulsating synthesizer note, evocative of a heartbeat, and Bono calling out for love one more time.

At this point, Bono recites the last lines of how the hands that build can also pull down, which serves, according to Adam, to symbolize the conflicts within America's domestic and foreign policies. [U2, *The Joshua Tree* liner notes] Larry's apocalyptic drums return with more intensity and the Edge launches into a longer solo with more barbarity than before. Thematically in the music, the first solo seems to signify the meeting between predator and prey, with the second solo playing out the act until its fatal completion. In the last 30 seconds, the synthesizer heartbeats return, but quieting and fading as each second goes by implying the victim's mortality fleeting and transitioning into lifelessness.

Even until the final day of recording, U2's proclivity for improvisation allowed them to create something with a style and delivery they had not been used to before, breaking new ground thematically and musically for the band. According to Adam, even when breaking down the different components of a jam session, they could ultimately lose the spirit and the concept goes nowhere, leaving behind mistakes and other technical issues. Though, he continues, often a song can be constructed so that it does not lose its energy and many of the issues inherent in the song become unnoticeable while the magic of the song remains intact and at the forefront. [McCormick and U2, *U2 by U2*, 184]

"Exit," recorded on the last day of the sessions and making it to the album final, does capture the spirit of *The Joshua Tree*, not only in terms of musical composition but also adding heft to the end point of one aspect of U2's existential journey through America. Up to this point, the band had seen America's faults and gifts, accentuating the elements of both while acknowledging the rift between them. With "Exit," sometimes falling into that rift, there is no escape.

Amid all of its flawed beauty, there is an underlying darkness in America as well as U2's relationship to it. In order to continue their journey in understanding a larger truth of America, U2 had to confront it in relation to examining their own inner darkness and what they had learned from the experience. The bigger picture of America they would come to understand and share through *The Joshua Tree*, as well as the pitfalls of newfound celebrity that could heighten their darker impulses, creates a potentially volatile situation that requires a consistent and ongoing self-conscious examination. While the figure in "Exit" is a manifestation of the darker impulses stemming from an inability to access the American Dream, too much access to it to the point of exploitation and excess presents its own risk of falling within the rift it creates. With this, U2 recognizes the full spectrum of their own humanity and strives to align with and elevate the best and brightest elements of it. Eamon Dunphy elucidates on this concept through his initial reaction to "Exit" in *Unforgettable Fire: Past, Present, and Future—The Definitive Biography of U2*, published in 1987, the same year as the release of *The Joshua Tree*. In the book, he says,

> Every stage of their journey has revealed a truth, about themselves or the times their music has attempted to reflect. The penultimate song on *The Joshua Tree* is "Exit." "Exit" means out from the confusion of the past, out of the twilight world where Christianity merge with rock 'n' roll to form doubt. That is over. U2 have exited into daylight, certain now that music is a gift from God and that as musicians their responsibility is to use it. Exposed by fame to temptations of the ego and the flesh on a scale that few people can imagine, their story is in essence just beginning. U2's greatest struggles lie ahead. [Dunphy, *Unforgettable Fire*, 281]

Disturbed by the darkened version of religion coopted by the figure in "Exit," U2 had to learn from their experiences and use those lessons from the past to shape a humanist vision of the future. Recording "Exit" may have purged them of the demon they encountered in the American heartland and, feeling cleansed of that evil, U2 could move forward emboldened by the belief America could be a country that can unite over fear. Though, the dichotomous rift through America is old as the country's sins itself, and the evils of man that exploit its darkness always return. U2 would discover that even exorcised demons can still haunt.

"Exit" had been played throughout The Joshua Tree tour in 1987 and only once during the Lovetown tour in Melbourne, Australia, in 1989. That year, Robert Bardo traveled from his home in Tucson, Arizona, to murder actress Rebecca Schaeffer, whom he had been stalking for several years. During the trial, Bardo and his lawyer insisted that "Exit" inspired him to carry out the murder. When the song was played in court, the Associated Press reported, "Bardo, who had sat glum and motionless through most of the trial, suddenly sprang to life. He grinned, bobbed up and down to the music, pounded his knee as if it was a drum and mouthed words to the song, including references to a gun." [Deutsch, "Obsessed Fan"]

Despite the connection between "Exit" and the Schaeffer murder, Bono had already distanced himself from the song before the details of Bardo's trial were known to U2. In an interview with *Musician* in 1993, Bono expressed that after performing "Exit," he just wanted to have a bath and wash the experience off. [Jackson, "Bono vs. The Beast"]

Though Bono claimed that U2 did not feel responsible for Bardo's actions, it is not clear if the murder itself was the primary reason why the band quit performing it live. On performing "Exit," Bono felt that as an artist, you have to follow where the music goes. By exploring the darker elements of the song within his imagination, Bono was able to experience the essence of the narrative without actually having to live it as a reality. He described the exploration as being able to take a walk through this darkness and sharing a pint with the Devil, but it wasn't a place he wanted to reside in. [Jackson, "Bono vs. The Beast"] Despite these thoughts about the darkness within U2's music, Bono said, referencing his own discomfort in performing the song on learning about Schaeffer's murder, that the event represented what happens when you cannot separate yourself from the Devil on this journey. [Jackson, "Bono vs. The Beast"]

By the time of The Joshua Tree Tour 2017, "Exit" would make its return in concert. Though, this time, Bono was not messing with the Devil; he embodied that Devil instead. With "Exit" being an intimate profile of a killer, Bono, while performing the song during the tour, embraced the killer within by acting out a persona called the "Shadow Man" created for this tour, a strange entity wearing a black suit and preacher hat that embodies the dark figure central to the song's narrative. In an interview with *Rolling Stone*, Bono discussed the significance of portraying the Shadow Man and returning to "Exit" for *The Joshua Tree*'s 30th anniversary. "Exit" had caused Bono much self-harm, and he was relieved in not playing it for so long. With "Exit," he was to venture into dark places during the performance. To separate himself emotionally and mentally from the song's sinister themes, Bono had to reframe the song within the context of the American literature he was exploring when initially writing it. Performing on stage, Bono stepped into the role of the Shadow Man, embodying a character that allowed him to distance himself from the song's dark and murderous narrative without experiencing the same self-harm he had endured before. As part of this performance, Bono recited, "Eenie, meenie, miny, moe," which has racist origins and connotations both in America and Europe. Bono, also as part of the character of the Shadow Man, recited the same lines Hazel Motes preached in O'Connor's novel: "Where you come from is gone. Where you thought you were going is never there. Where you are is no good unless you can get away from it." [Greene, "Bono Talks"]

With the resurgence of "Exit" on The Joshua Tree Tour 2017, U2 also modernized their messaging of the song as a critique of US policy and applied it to Trump in a clever way. Right before the band began "Exit," the stage projection screened a video clip from *Trackdown*, a western television series that ran from 1957 to 1959 on CBS, in which a man named Walter Trump aims to con the people of a small town. Trump ensures the townsfolk that he is the only man capable of building a wall to keep out foreigners and invaders, thus guaranteeing the safety of the town and its citizens. With the presence of Trump and his empty promises, the townspeople clash, with some believing Trump's promises and others dismissing Trump as a liar. Although this clip from *Trackdown*, due to when it was produced, was likely an expression of criticism against Fred Trump, the controversial New York real estate developer and father of Donald, its use within the context of the 2017 tour made it clear it was meant to address the current president and his promises to keep migrants out of America through his plans to construct a wall along the US–Mexico border. As the clip played, Adam began the bass opening for "Exit," illustrating the song's connection to a critique of America's own destructive policies.

The space "Exit" occupies on *The Joshua Tree* is one that is austere and bleak but served a necessary purpose. The band recognized that confronting something that stands in your way means also reconciling, or at the very least recognizing, those same traces within yourself. Although America can be a hopeful place, it is also harboring an evil the country fails or, perhaps, refuses to resolve. In order to ascend toward the light of the beacon of hope and liberty they had initially believed America to be, U2 first had to immerse themselves into total darkness.

Chapter Six

She Is Liberty

As U2 explored America, the desert became a source of inspiration and fascination for the band as they reflected on the American Dream and the failure of the construct. Although the desert served as the backdrop for several songs on *The Joshua Tree*, the band further explored the imagery of arid landscapes, and the people within them, as a textural element to find broken beauty as a reflection of mystery and spirituality. Adam believed that many dismiss the desert as being a desolate wasteland, but when recording *The Joshua Tree*, it came to represent something more positive and ideal for U2. The desert imagery presented itself as a blank canvas for the band to explore their musical ideas, reframing the perception of the desert being barren and void of life into something more creatively constructive. [Parkyn, *U2 Touch the Flame*, 78]

The blank canvas of a desert landscape was a perfect opportunity to add a thematic character to *The Joshua Tree* that elevated the album's narrative addressing the many aspects of the American Dream. How to convey the spiritual and emotional essence of the desert was unclear at the beginning. Crafting an ode to an iconic American landscape and how it played into the American Dream was something that had to be deeply felt. Ahead of U2 was an enigma that they could not explain, but they could praise and admire the desert's complexities as wayfarers searching for truth.

This textured ode to the western landscape of America would eventually result in the track "In God's Country" and was born out of U2's process of improvisation. According to Bono, U2 had never historically written songs in any traditional sense. As part of their process, they would develop a collaborative sound and shape it further through improvisational jamming, its textural qualities informing the lyrics. [Black, *Bono in His Own Words*, 39] This improvisational method allowed U2 to focus primarily on the music and then find the appropriate image to add meaning to the music.

Recording the music for "In God's Country" was challenging. Adam said recording the song was difficult despite the simplicity of the composition, describing it as a "throwaway piece." Recognizing that U2 were not professionally trained musicians, having created their music through jamming together as friends and bandmates, Adam said that "In God's Country" revealed their limitations at the time. U2's goal when recording was to find the balance between making music that engrossed them and music that worked within their vision, with Adam describing that "In God's Country" was stuck in between. The Edge echoed Adam's thoughts, suggesting that the band acknowledged that "In God's Country" would never be one of their greatest songs, but they needed to add some up-tempo tracks to the album. [McCormick and U2, *U2 by U2*, 182]

The band's lack of training spurred tension within the group. The journey to explore and expose America's dichotomy was creating its own rift within the group as U2 recorded "In God's Country." The unease and agitation they were sensing in America took the band to new places where they were not so guarded, reflecting those feelings during the process of recording the song. While recording "In God's Country," Bono became frustrated with the Edge and tried to get him to deliver a more rock-and-roll style. So Bono, despite being considerably inexperienced with guitar compared with the Edge, showed him an A-minor to D sequence. The Edge told Bono that his guitar playing was crap and, motivated by his own competitive spirit, performed something that was an improvement. [McCormick and U2, *U2 by U2*, 182]

The scene in the recording studio became increasingly tense while recording "In God's Country." Larry recalled the Edge generally behaved as if in a competition, noting that he would listen to other guitarists until he could discern how they were playing and how they achieved their effects. This drove him to become engrossed in the full spectrum of a guitar's sound capability and the soundscape he could craft from it. Larry described that the Edge's competitiveness, although being integral to U2's overall music aesthetic, usually came from his frustration from Bono's comparatively weaker skill as a guitar player. [McCormick and U2, *U2 by U2*, 182]

"In God's Country" is notably unlike much of the other material on *The Joshua Tree*. Not only is it the shortest song on the album, the only one clocking in at less than three minutes, but it is also the one with the least cohesion in terms of narrative lyricism. Even Bono, who wrote the lyrics, has difficulty determining where the song came from, saying he was eventually unsure if he was writing about either America or Ireland. [White, *Rock Stars*]

While much of the song deals with desert imagery, the conflation between the US and Irish experiences Bono was juggling can be explained with the line about needing new dreams. *The Joshua Tree* is U2's exploration of the promised land of America by Irishmen, only to find out the reality and broken dreams it actually contains were not much different from their experiences growing up. Regarding Bono's songwriting for the album, the Edge said that the songs were all relative to their growing fascination with America and that the band did not fully understand and appreciate their own Irishness until they left

Ireland. Through this exploration of America, and the growing sense of alienation they felt along the journey, they became aware of the different aspects that made up America's complex identity. [Parkyn, *U2 Touch the Flame*, 81]

Within "In God's Country," Bono sings of dreamers dying every day to capture a glimpse of what is happening on the other side of their own existence and describes those who seek a better life for themselves. Regarding U2's journey to understand their own heritage within America, this further blurs the line between the struggles the Irish historically knew and the inhabitants of America's desert communities, like the people in the song, who live on the fringes of US society, seeking prosperity and opportunities. Both groups have a desire for salvation that will bring them a better life, one founded within the principles of the promised American Dream. Instead, these forgotten souls exist, as Bono sings, as having sad eyes looking toward a crooked cross, a symbol of redemption and sacrifice, while eagerly awaiting sleep where they are satiated with the comforting salve of their own dreams and desires. Bono sings of sleep as a drug; a means to escape the reality of their own existence and the endless search for more. Without the drug of sleep, these dreamers will never fully be satisfied because of the artifice of the American Dream promised to them by those in power who control wealth. A devastating cycle of emotional cruelty perpetrated by the widening of America's dichotomous rift at the hands of its own government.

"In God's Country" is the connection between America and Ireland, suggesting that America is, and continues to remain, a strong lure for the people of Ireland. For Adam, the generations of Irish being fascinated with America stems from the experiences of those who fled to the new world to find hope. He believes that America's own vastness resonated deeply with the Irish who sought to flourish within it because of the physical and geographical challenges and limitations they faced back home. [Rock Express, "Soul of America"]

For Bono, reflecting on the desert landscape and him connecting the plight of the Irish to that of Americans in the heartland of their country, "In God's Country" became another song on *The Joshua Tree* to make a statement about the failure of the American Dream. While "Bullet the Blue Sky" was a fiery condemnation and "Mothers of the Disappeared" was a somber prayer, "In God's Country" embodied an abstract emotional response personifying the concept of a group of people left behind by their country. In 1989, Bono told *Mother Jones* his thoughts on the ambiguity and complexities of what he was feeling when writing "In God's Country," saying,

> I have this feeling of starting over, that things have reached their end, and also this notion that while people always talk about being joined in common wants and aspirations, I'm finding the reverse. Finding we're united in desperation. I dunno, I come back to that line from our song "In God's Country": "We need new dreams tonight." The job is to dream up a world you'd want to live in. [Block, "Bono Bites Back"]

In a 1987 radio interview with Timothy White, Bono explained that he was writing in dedication to the Statue of Liberty. [White, *Rock Stars*] The dedication is evident in the lyrics and their inherent symbolism. In *Into the Heart*, Niall Stokes describes Bono's lyrics suggesting that they came "to him in a dream, the USA is characterized as a desert rose, a siren whose dress is torn and in bows." [Stokes, *Into the Heart*, 72] The desert rose, a metaphor for the Statue of Liberty, calls to Bono with a siren's song. The Statue of Liberty, a symbol of opportunity and prosperity, is what these dreamers see when they close their eyes. In their dreams, she is coming to rescue them with hope and faith as well as gold, symbolizing prosperity as the greatest gift they could receive and as a means to escape their own desperation. Though, reflecting on

"In God's Country," Bono cautions the dreamers asking them whether this woman has come to save them or if she is really a siren drawing them toward their demise. [White, *Rock Stars*] Such a question expands U2's critique of America and adds complexity to the allure, and potential drawback, of hoping for salvation from those in power who are responsible for their oppression.

At the end of the song, Bono sings that this supposed figure of salvation holds a naked flame with Bono standing among these dreamers described by him as the sons of Cain, the biblical figure in the Book of Genesis who murdered his brother Abel because God favored Abel's sacrifices more than Cain's. As being among the sons of Cain, Bono is suggesting that he shares an understanding and connection with those born with the sins of the father, and the fallout stemming from an element of the human condition that people with the same beliefs can still be enemies due to an inherent aversion to equality. In the last line, this naked flame the figure holds, a nod to the Statue of Liberty and her torch, burns Bono and the sons of Cain with its love. This final line in the song evokes the duality of America as a symbol of both salvation and damnation, representing the cultural and social dichotomy of America. The Statue of Liberty's role in "In God's Country" ties back in with the song being part of *The Joshua Tree*'s overall critique of America and the underlying beauty of the desert as a seemingly desolate place. The mysterious allure of the desert as an image, according to the Edge, reflected *The Joshua Tree*'s spiritual tone. [Stokes, *Into the Heart*, 72] The Edge connecting the desert with spirituality suggests a level of transcendence that certainly aligns with Adam's comments about finding beauty with the right frame of mind. If "In God's Country" serves as a metaphorical response to the Reagan administration's politics and the enabling of a wealthy fundamentalist elite, the desert becomes overwhelming in its seemingly spiritless dreariness. Though, if you look closer and concentrate on its subtle beauty, the rose hidden in the wasteland serves as a beacon of optimism that life can rise out of desolation. Though the song profiles a forgotten people who are lost in a harsh environment, there is still a semblance of hope. The question is whether this hope is misplaced or there is something greater to yearn for.

In the interview with White, Bono continued explaining the meaning behind "In God's Country." The desert was a metaphor for stifling neoconservative politics that represented an archaic way of thinking that further divided the country. Instead, Bono suggested, America had to be held accountable and to ensure the American Dream was available to everyone, seeking to write a song that explored the yearning for the American Dream. [White, *Rock Stars*] Bono then suggested that the future of the country, through the promise of a rose breaking through the dry landscape, is up to the dreamers he referenced in the song. Dismissing the outdated ideologies of Reagan, he wondered where the new dreamers are. He yearned for new dreams in the song and desired for a new wave of people to overthrow outdated ideals for bold, progressive ones.

Although narratively and compositionally different from the other songs on *The Joshua Tree*, and dismissed by the band during the time of recording, "In God's Country" serves its own purpose for the album. Musically and lyrically, it adds a unique texture that is not captured by most of the other songs on the album. Although some songs are about specific injustices and others explore spirituality or personal feelings within the band, "In God's Country" is the only song on the record to focus on the cinematic and elemental qualities of a landscape, which serves as the backdrop for much of the album. Actions, narratives, and characters at the forefront of desert scenes play out in other parts of *The Joshua Tree*, but "In God's Country" evokes the setting with all the subtle detail that goes into it while adding depth to the adversities and triumphs of the album's narrative qualities as a whole. It provides a sense of atmosphere by establishing a location as a character in itself where the album's message is most effective—a seemingly desolate region teeming with life on the fringes.

During The Joshua Tree and Lovetown tours, "In God's Country" was frequently performed but later dismissed with the exception of a few performances and snippets over the years since 1989. This was largely due to the problems the song created for the Edge who felt unable to perform sonically on the same level as Bono's vocals. Despite its inclusion on *The Joshua Tree*, "In God's Country" just did not work for U2 beyond the scope of the album.

To commemorate *The Joshua Tree*'s 30th anniversary, "In God's Country" was performed every night on The Joshua Tree Tour 2017. During the performances, Bono spoke to the crowd and drew a connection between the physical characteristics of a vinyl record with those of the landscape represented in "In God's Country," discussing the nature of a vinyl record and the experience that comes from the dropping of the needle onto the grooves and hearing the scratches and music. Introducing a song about a location by admiring the physicality of the music's medium emphasized the importance of physical space, not just within the themes of *The Joshua Tree*, but also its role in our lives from the subtle to the obvious. [U2, Rome concert]

Before starting the song, Bono spoke to the audience about U2's journey over 30 years and learning how to properly play their own songs live. "In God's Country," being a song they were frustrated with while recording, is one of those songs that took three decades to play properly in a way that gave the song life and meaning within a live setting. Revisiting the song to confront that frustration again, in 2017, signified a return to the landscape that was a source of mystery and admiration for the band.

In that return to the desert landscape, an important part of the experience was to see what had changed over the course of 30 years when "In God's Country" initially addressed Reagan politics. Bono talked about America's need to live up to the idea it portrays to the rest of the world, and during a show in Rome on July 16, 2017, Bono said "In God's Country" is a song that represents America not just as a country but rather an idea that everyone has a stake in. Continuing, Bono declared that he wants this idea of America, a promise, to come true and succeed. [U2, Rome concert]

Though Bono did not specifically mention Trump during the monologue prior to performing "In God's Country," that is exactly who he was speaking about. In their return to the heart of the song, U2 recognized how Trump's lies and behavior alienated the people most at risk of the false hopes he promised. Bono believes this alienation stemmed from a mourning of a lost innocence in America, resulting from many Americans expressing their grievances with political institutions in the form of seeking salvation from a figure that did not represent their interests. [Greene, "Bono on How"]

The mourning Bono speaks about is reminiscent of the sad eyes of the people in "In God's Country" who long for the druglike effects of sleep as a form of escape from reality. This was due to the naivete many Americans felt regarding the future of the country. People were either incredulous at the idea of Trump's brand of nationalist populism achieving the presidency, or they believed Trump could save the country from economic ruin and perceived foreign threats. Within this context, he was the siren calling toward the people of America. U2's issue was that Trump exploited both sides of the political spectrum in ways that accentuated the widening gap of an already dichotomous America. Now, the people manipulated by Trump were searching for their desert rose to deliver salvation. The only question now, with the existential crisis the country faces that exacerbates its dichotomy, is if a rose can bloom through the scars of Trump's desert landscape—a beautiful notion but one with thorns.

CHAPTER SEVEN

Touch the Flame

U2's LANDMARK PERFORMANCE AT LIVE AID IN 1985 PRESENTED opportunities for the band and, specifically, Bono to pursue humanitarian causes in developing countries. It is during these humanitarian missions that Bono started to think more about the conceptual framework of *The Joshua Tree*, the existential journey through a complex landscape to seek something of greater worth that may never be found but is worthy of hope. Although this theme would evolve during the recording of *The Joshua Tree* to include an admonishment of America for its inherent dichotomy and political exploitation, these humanitarian missions allowed Bono to introspectively think about his own life and privilege.

Invited by World Vision, a Christian organization focused on relief initiatives, Bono and his wife Ali spent a month in Ethiopia where they witnessed firsthand the starvation that ravaged the area. Steve Reynolds, the director for World Vision, had discussed with Bono that his involvement with support in Ethiopia would not be a way to hype the organization as a celebrity public relations stunt. Reynolds' assurances that Bono would be volunteering as a normal citizen instead of the front man for an up-and-coming rock band was attractive for Bono and ultimately convinced him to go. [McCormick and U2, *U2 by U2*, 167] Without telling anyone, Bono and Ali went on a mission and volunteered at a camp providing aid and food for refugees as well as performing songs to teach children lessons about basic hygiene. Bono later recalled how shocking, and ultimately humbling, it was to see thousands of Ethiopians at the camp dressed in rags. Many who came for help were denied entry and food, due to the limited resources, yet they watched as others ate while expressing no animosity toward them. [McCormick and U2, *U2 by U2*, 167] In an interview with Michka Assayas, Bono said,

> In the morning as the mist would lift we would see thousands of people walking in lines toward the camp, people who had been walking for great distances through the night . . . Some as they got to the camp would collapse. Some would leave their children at the gates and some would leave their dead children at the fences to be buried. [Assayas, *Bono*, 246–47]

It was an experience in which Bono would witness devastation and systemic aspects of the area's poverty firsthand, a realization that not only war and environmental issues were causes of famine and starvation but also corruption within African governments as well as their trade agreements with the most developed nations. [McCormick and U2, *U2 by U2*, 167–69] At a time when U2 were earning their place on the world stage as the next big thing in rock music, this opportunity to volunteer in Ethiopia gave Bono time to step away from that lifestyle and think about how his life was changing and ways to use his new platform to shed light on global inequality. "Whether it was Live Aid, the anti-apartheid movement or Amnesty International, music was now seen as a unifying force," said Bono in *U2 by U2*, "a kind of glue to make a new political constituency." [McCormick and U2, *U2 by U2*, 169]

In his book, *U2: Rock 'N' Roll To Change The World*, Timothy D. Neufeld discusses how, despite the starvation and devastation these Ethiopians suffered, "there was a beauty to the place, a rich culture filled with strong and noble people" and Bono, during his mission work with World Vision, saw "an enduring spirit in the laughter and smiles of the Ethiopians." [Neufeld, *U2*, 57] This juxtaposition of these people starving but still finding joy despite their struggle for survival, living in the stunning yet often unforgiving landscape of an African desert, gave Bono the inspiration for the imagery and themes for what would become *The Joshua Tree*. While the critique of a dichotomous America would be incorporated later on as the album continued to develop, Bono's trip to Ethiopia set the groundwork for the album to be an introspective look at the complexities of the relationship one has with themselves and how they fit in within humanity's relationship with its environment. Setting the stage as the album opener, "Where the Streets Have No Name" would be the epic introduction in which the listener would embark with U2 on their existential journey through America.

Before writing the song, the early stages of the development of *The Joshua Tree* also stemmed from Bono being fascinated by the biblical concept of the desert as a setting. In an interview with *Rolling Stone*, Bono described the early lyrical sketches he was writing during his mission in Ethiopia. Writing on airplane sick bags and various scraps of paper, Bono sketched ideas about deserts within the larger context of a parched earth while staying in a tent in the northern Ethiopian town Ajibar. For Bono at the time, these rough lyrical sketches remained unclear outside of the African context, but he was drawn to the spirit and energy of the idea. For him, God is met in the desert because during times of drought and difficulty, one discovers who they are when encountering God. [Wenner, 2005 interview]

The powerful idea that Bono was trying to convey out of the African context results in one of the most interesting qualities of "Where the Streets Have No Name": the vagueness of the song's lyrics and intended meaning. For the listener, there is an uncertainty as to where exactly Bono is singing about whether it be an actual location, an ethereal or heavenly plane of existence, or even a frame of mind. There is an openness that allows listeners to ascertain potentially their own meaning, interpreting what this place is for Bono or for themselves. Speaking to *Propaganda* in 1987, Bono explained that the song resembled U2's earlier songs more than it did the others on *The Joshua Tree* because it is the one song on the album that most heavily relied on sketched ideas, as opposed to a clearer and more refined theme or narrative. Bono expressed wanting to break out of the claustrophobia he was feeling in the urban jungle and his yearning to go somewhere where he was not held back by modern society. With "Where the Streets Have No Name," evoking perhaps a spiritual location, Bono wanted to capture what he was feeling. [*Propaganda*, "The Joshua Tree"]

On albums prior to *The Joshua Tree*, Bono would sketch lyrics since he believed words were, at the time, not important in making rock music. It was during the recording of *The Joshua Tree* that Bono, pushed by the other members of U2, would take time to learn the craft of songwriting to write better and more fully realized lyrics. As a result, it is a richly conceptualized album that evokes feelings and responses to specific ideas central to the album's larger theme, the American dichotomy through a foreigner's eyes. Hence, it is curious how "Where the Streets Have No Name" was conceived to be written with such a lack of clarity yet was chosen to open the album. Although it is true that the song, as Bono described, resembles earlier songs than its counterparts on *The Joshua Tree*, that is only in terms of the song's lyrical sketch style. Thematically, despite the song's meaning being seemingly less obvious than others on the album, "Where the Streets Have No Name" fits and, even, introduces the album's theme of critiquing the US dichotomy and how the country's policies negatively impact the lives of its citizens and those around the world.

Because the inspiration for the song came from Bono's trip to Ethiopia, it is often assumed that "Where the Streets Have No Name" was about Ethiopian streets where allegedly the streets were numbered instead of named. In actuality, the song was initially written to include Bono's recent understanding of the inequality of people in Northern Ireland as a reflection of Western society as a whole. Bono discussed the song's origin with *Propaganda* in 1987, saying it stemmed from a story once told to him. In Belfast, you could figure out someone's religious denominations or their economic class based on what street they lived on—even down to which side of the street their house was on—because the class and social lines in Belfast were so well-defined. This spoke to Bono and his desire of needing to capture a spiritual feeling and location that he sought to write about a place where the streets have no name, effectively erasing these societal demarcations he was hearing about. [*Propaganda*, "The Joshua Tree"]

Though initially attributed to the economic and social inequities in Belfast, Bono has since strayed away from that notion over the years. In a 2000 interview with 2CR FM, Bono added a broader layer to the song's original meaning by saying he used to think it was about Belfast. [2CR FM, interview] What Bono describes about the song and the concept of how one's value and identity is determined by where they live is applicable to all of Western society and, when considering the larger themes of *The Joshua Tree*, addresses America's issues with inequality as it relates to its dichotomy. During the 1980s, neoconservative fiscal policies, championed by the Reagan administration, widened the wealth disparity between the wealthy and the poor. With cuts to various aid and social welfare programs, Reagan was advancing class disparities in a way that it was obvious who was adversely affected and who benefited. The desert imagery in the song becomes the cinematic landscape in which to illustrate a physical representation of this dichotomy, a harsh and brutal environment where people struggle to thrive. Bono recalled that the people he met in Ethiopia were strong in spirit and felt that, despite the poverty they were enduring, they had something that he was missing, something deeper and more spiritual. The experience he had in Ethiopia led Bono to believe that Western civilization was behaving like rotten and self-indulgent children. [Stokes, "Greatest Songs"]

Although the origin of "Where the Streets Have No Name" criticized the economic and social realities of Western society, the song's narrative is one of escape. While listeners were left wondering if the song was about a real place, it is actually about an idea: a hopeful place, with Bono envisioning desert plains, where the societal divisions of race, class, religion, ethnicity, gender, or any form used to discriminate against other people are nonexistent, a place of love and equality. For Bono, it was a conceptual framework to determine the kind of world he envisioned for Western society, especially America. "Where the Streets Have No Name" represents a vision of a place to escape to that is rid of all forms of social inequities. Within the scope of *The Joshua Tree*, it is a yearning for what America could be, what it is promised to be.

As a vision for a more equitable world, the song also represents another form of escape. The trip to Ethiopia, which was done relatively in secret, gave Bono a chance to delve into that anonymity he was seeking after U2's increased fame following Live Aid. In addition to setting the scene for a critique of America, this place where the streets have no name was also a way for Bono to come to terms with the life changes of being a rock star. Bono sings about a desire to run and to hide, to tear down walls, and touch the flame of this mythical place, a place where he can just exist as himself. In *Into the Heart*, Niall Stokes suggests that "Where the Streets Have No Name" "expresses the corresponding desire to cut and run, but it also captures the desperate need for anonymity that someone in Bono's position frequently feels." [Stokes, *Into the Heart*, 64] Bono was struggling with new ideas that challenged his conceptions of society and privilege, a state of being he described as blending the notion of being both a hunter and a guardian. Within the context of the album, this desire of escape reflects the internal struggle one faces when their preconceived notions of America are far more complex than originally believed. Therein lies the decision to challenge America and expose its hypocrisies or to merely ignore them. As the album's opener, the song reveals the challenges and desire of taking the first steps toward an existential journey through America and the internal conflict that comes with it.

Within the narrative of *The Joshua Tree* being a critique of America's dichotomy, "Where the Streets Have No Name" represents U2's hope for the country to live up to its ideals as a promised land. The mythos of America that the band had grown up with in Ireland, one of the poorest countries in Western Europe at that time, represented an idea they sought for themselves as a place to escape to. It was also something many Americans, often those adversely affected by Reagan's policies, desired as they continued to struggle against systemic inequality inherent within their own country's structure. This idea, a promised land, becomes essential as a motivation to stay hopeful that, someday, there will be equality. Juxtaposing this inequality with the anonymity he experienced visiting Ethiopia, Bono wrote the song to illustrate the stark contrasts that make up the world's inequities. For Bono, where there are no such social artifices and divisions is a place where people can come together, like a rock concert that tears down the barriers dividing people and illustrates what really matters such as the commonalties we all share. [Hilburn, "U2's Bono Hewson"]

While the band was taking a break from *The Joshua Tree* recording sessions, the music for "Where the Streets Have No Name" originated as a demo by the Edge who was seeking to "conjure up the ultimate U2 live-song." Reflecting on recording the demo in *U2 by U2*, the Edge recalled becoming anxious about U2's next tour as he diligently worked, unaccompanied by the rest of the band, sequencing the keyboards to the drum machine onto a four-track tape machine, driving him to consider how he wanted U2 to sound when playing the new songs in concert. When the rough mix was finished, the Edge celebrated by dancing around the room, amazed after coming up with the guitar part that would become the signature intro of "Where the Streets Have No Name." [McCormick and U2, *U2 by U2*, 184–85]

In the studio, recording "Where the Streets Have No Name" became a Sisyphean effort for U2. In an interview with *Hot Press*, Lanois compared the track to a science project and recalled deconstructing the song on a large blackboard, illustrating the song's characteristics and chord changes as if he were leading a college lecture. [O'Hare, "The Secret History"] What made recording it so difficult was the song's chord changes. The introduction is played in a three-quarter time signature, then transitions into a four-quarter time signature, then reverts back to three-quarter time for the song's outro, all at a tempo of 126 beats per minute.

Adam had doubts that the band could play the song despite an excellent sounding demo. Recording the track was a new challenge for them because, unlike their process of improvisational jamming for other songs, they could not make sense of the structure of the song and its numerous time shifts and chord changes. Adam recalled the band would continuously rehearse and perform the song in the studio but felt as though they were not getting any closer to a final take. The final version that would end up on *The Joshua Tree* compiled elements and takes from different recordings. [McCormick and U2, *U2 by U2*, 185]

Perhaps the most notorious anecdote from *The Joshua Tree* recording sessions was that the tape for "Where the Streets Have No Name" was almost erased by Eno, frustrated with time spent recording the song, by creating a staged accident in which the song would be recorded over. According to *Classic Albums*, engineer Pat McCarthy allegedly found Eno cueing the tape for erasure, dropped his tea, and was forced to restrain Eno from recording over the tape. Eno, in response to the legendary story, justified his action by rationalizing it would have been easier to start the song from scratch because Eno, Lanois, and the band were spending weeks recording "Where the Streets Have No Name." According to Eno, half the time spent producing the album was spent on recording the one song. Admitting it can be a daunting ordeal to start over, he felt it was better to begin again with nothing. His plan to erase the tape was part of an orchestrated accident so the band would be forced to start fresh as opposed to hammering out the song's nuances that Eno felt were holding the band back from finishing the album. [*Classic Albums, The Joshua Tree*]

The Edge's goal for "Where the Streets Have No Name" was to create the ultimate live U2 song. While the studio version of the song is considered to be one of U2's most beloved within their discography, the band recognized it contained less energy than the live performances of the song. Larry recalled that the greatness of "Where the Streets Have No Name" comes from the live performances as opposed to the album version, believing that the process of recording the song was too arduous for the band to really understand. [McCormick and U2, *U2 by U2*, 185]

Though, U2 did succeed in crafting the song to be an experience best enjoyed in concert as a representation of the power and magnitude of their live performances. Since its debut on April 2, 1987, during the opening of The Joshua Tree tour, "Where the Streets Have No Name" has become a live staple in almost all of U2's tours since. According to *AtU2*, a U2 fan site launched in 1995 and operated until shutting down in 2020, the song had been performed more than 900 times as of 2020 and is a fan favorite. In Višnja Cogan's *U2: An Irish Phenomenon*, Bono recognized the song's legacy as U2's definitive live song, saying that the song could elevate the concert experience even if they were performing the worst show of their career because it brought the audience out of the seats singing along with every word in a way, as Bono suggested, as if God had just entered the room. [Cogan, *U2*, 110] Clearly the song and its narrative of escape resonates well with U2's fans and audiences.

During The Joshua Tree Tour 2017, U2 modernized the song to reflect a collective journey with the audience. Following "Pride (In the Name of Love)" in the set, Bono spoke during the synthesizer introduction about Dr. Martin Luther King Jr. and the previous song's praising of his peaceful ideals, segueing into "Where the Streets Have No Name" while bridging the two songs thematically. Over the signature synthesizer introduction, Bono would call out to Dr. King for guidance to keep themselves and the audience tolerant in times of terror and to strengthen their faith in justice and community during times of fear. [U2, Rome concert] In this context, Bono reinforced *The Joshua Tree*'s critique of America and the threat that Trump's policies posed to the ideals of Dr. King, and that they and others can be impacted if they lose sight of Dr. King's vision.

At the end of the song's introduction, just before Bono sang the vocals, the video projection screen transitioned from a silhouette of a Joshua tree over a bright red background to a black-and-white video of a highway running through a desert landscape. The camera went down the highway through the desert, passing migrants walking along the shoulder carrying backpacks and jugs of water. This video signified the modern contextualization of "Where the Streets Have No Name" in the Trump era. The meaning of the song is one of escape, searching for a place that breaks down society's divisions. With Trump's violent rhetoric against migrants and refugees, most notably calling for a wall along the US–Mexico border and locking migrant children in cages, he actively denied them freedom to seek asylum and refuge, to run and hide from the poison rain of inequality.

In an interview with Beats 1, now Apple Music, regarding the 30th anniversary of *The Joshua Tree*, Bono discussed his feelings on "Where the Streets Have No Name" as an unfinished song. "Half of it is an invocation," Bono said, "where you say to a crowd of people 'Do you want to go to that place? That place of imagination, that place of soul?

Do you want to go there, cos right now we can go there?' To this day when I say those words you get hairs on the back of your neck stand up because you're going to that place." [Apple Music, interview] The unfinished element of the song is the journey U2 wants the audience to join them on toward its idealized destination. In this, Bono is saying that this journey to a place that breaks down society's inequities is one that we can all take together, especially during a toxic political climate where freedoms for the marginalized members of society are most at risk. Although it is essential that we seek the place where the streets have no name for ourselves, we do have a larger responsibility to make that journey as a civilization, as a community.

Bono sings of a desolate place where people are blown by the wind and beaten down into dust. The harshness and brutality of an unforgiving desert landscape inherent in the song's imagery is visualized on the screen to illustrate the obstacles people overcome to seek refuge, something Bono witnessed firsthand in Ethiopia. With Trump's dangerous and racist policies toward immigrants, the inherent themes of "Where the Streets Have No Name" are apparent as being global and indicative of a desire all people share: to seek equality and dignity. Bono did not have to mention Trump for this performance to be effective. It is effective through its visual and lyrical imagery and the inclusion of the entire audience on this journey. By changing the song's original first-person perspective to sing that we, the band as well as the audience, can go to where the streets have no name, the song became a humanistic declaration of the journey we all must take as a society to break down our divisions.

CHAPTER EIGHT

Angel or Devil

DURING THEIR EXISTENTIAL JOURNEY THROUGH AMERICA TO RECORD *The Joshua Tree*, U2 became fascinated with American folk and blues music. Part of this was a desire for U2 to discover new musical avenues that would give them something fresh to explore and apply to their own growing musical sensibilities. They had no desire to sound like anything directly inspired by a particular genre or musical movement, but they needed something to stimulate their creativity and allow them to continue on their journey exploring America.

Despite such a strong motivation to reflect their newfound fascination with American roots music, this desire to put blues and folk through U2's sonic filter would result in another song the band and critics would at times dismiss as a throwaway piece. Although "In God's Country" was initially considered by the band as a throwaway despite adding a cinematic landscape to the album, "Trip Through Your Wires" could be at first hearing considered as another throwaway lyrically, but it captures a raw essence of American roots music while upholding the overall narrative of the album.

Niall Stokes outlines the history of the development of "Trip Through Your Wires" in *Into the Heart* by connecting U2's drive to find a way to express America's musical past with what was happening in the music scene in Ireland during the 1980s. Stokes suggests that Bono likely conceived the musical direction that would become "Trip Through Your Wires" after seeing groups like The Waterboys and Hothouse Flowers busking around Dublin combining elements of Irish folk tradition with the style of American folk icons like Bob Dylan. [Stokes, *Into the Heart*, 73]

It was during Bono's search for musical inspiration that he was approached by Billy Magra, a friend who was a producer for the RTE program *TV Gaga*. As a favor, Bono agreed that U2 would perform two new songs. At this point, U2 were in the early stages of planning the album concept for their follow-up to *The Unforgettable Fire*. They did not know exactly what they wanted to do, but the goal was to add some American elements. They had barely even begun writing songs for the next album when the commitment was made to play fresh material.

That night in 1986, viewers in Ireland got a taste of the new direction U2 was taking. Stokes described the band as "looking like extras from some B-movie remake of *Easy Rider*" as they launched into their three-song set. The first song performed was a new original composition called "Woman Fish," a chunky number that featured Bono emulating the vocal delivery of Black Southern blues singers backed by a frantically generic postpunk guitar courtesy of the Edge. The song abandoned after its debut with the footage never again to see the light of day until the arrival of YouTube.

The next song was an early version of "Trip Through Your Wires" featuring distinctly different lyrics in this early draft of the song. A rhythm-and-blues romp straight out of an American honky-tonk, it was the earliest component of the direction U2 wanted to go in that would eventually make it on the final album, although with newer lyrics and dramatic production changes by Eno and Lanois.

Closing the set, to really play up this new American direction for the Irish viewers, U2 performed an awkward cover of Bob Dylan's "Knockin'

On Heaven's Door." This bewildering cover performance featured Bono delivering an impromptu spoken word monologue, his own modified version of Dylan's lyrics, an added verse unironically singing "I don't know the words and sometimes I don't know the tune" along with the melody, and strangely calling out Reagan before launching into the chorus again. In *U2 by U2*, the Edge said that it was during a "moment of dementia" that they agreed to perform these unfinished songs for a live television audience. For him, performing these unpolished early drafts of songs for their next album was the worst moment to showcase U2's new creative and musical direction [McCormick and U2, *U2 by U2*, 172]

On the version that would make it to the album, the harmonica on "Trip Through Your Wires" is the signature musical element of the track. Although rougher during the RTE performance that likely started as Bono overstating just how American U2's new direction was, the use of it on *The Joshua Tree* adds life and spontaneity to what would just otherwise be a polished jam session. Bono performed harmonica for the song despite having very little experience with it, often considering himself a poor harmonica player. Since then, it is a musical touchstone Bono brings out on rare occasions in concert. [McCormick and U2, *U2 by U2*, 184]

Despite Bono's assertion that he is a poor harmonica player, the other members of U2 would disagree with Bono's take on his harmonica skills. Larry described Bono as being a decent harmonica player, while Adam said Bono could deliver an aggressiveness with his playing. [McCormick and U2, *U2 by U2*, 182] The harmonica, despite the other qualities of the song, is truly the saving grace of the track, and it gives "Trip Through Your Wires" a musical character synonymous with the rugged danger of the American Southwest. That track, with its bluesy barroom style, adds a missing texture to the overall portrait of America that showcases the country's ability to roll with the punches and have a good time despite troubles.

John Jobling described "Trip Through Your Wires" as "a drunken, blues harp-filled romp that evoked the rough-and-tumble spirit of Bob Dylan's *The Basement Tapes*. Production-wise, it was the epitome of the organic, band-in-a-room sound U2 was striving for." [Jobling, *U2*, 163] Bono described U2 playing the song in the studio as becoming a big hootenanny that captured the spirit of the moment, encouraged by Eno and Lanois to generate ideas from performing impromptu jams. In the midst of this jam session during the early stage of recording "Trip Through Your Wires" in the studio, Lanois would play tambourine and inspire the band to get lost in the moment and magic of the sessions. [Stokes, *Into the Heart*, 74] It was a thrill for Bono but also represented how their ideas were often influenced by *The Joshua Tree*'s producers when the band was too caught up in themselves and stuck with an idea.

Although "Trip Through Your Wires" is indeed fun and adds a distinct feel to the overall theme of *The Joshua Tree* identifying and highlighting a multifaceted America whose dichotomous nature is growing, it was an odd choice for the album considering the quality of the other material U2 recorded during *The Joshua Tree* sessions. The original concept Bono proposed was to make a double album, one disc focused more on American blues and folk music and the other continuing the European sound U2 had been known for on their four previous albums. A decision was ultimately made, and the band pursued the American concept with enthusiasm and curiosity, unsure of what they would find on their journey.

Reflecting on *The Joshua Tree*'s 30th anniversary, *Rolling Stone* interviewed the Edge in 2017, and he discussed the role American roots music played in the creation of the album. The punk rock traditions that U2 originated from typically sought to create music that was not influenced by American music, instead focusing on creating music that was unparalleled and unique. Citing U2's previous records, the Edge acknowledged the influence then contemporary German music had on the band as well as other bands in the United Kingdom. When writing and recording *The Joshua Tree*, the Edge recalled that there was a conscious decision to move away from Europe as musical inspiration to explore the roots of the American music that they were being drawn to. [Greene, "The Edge"]

Although U2 did record enough music for a double album, *The Joshua Tree* would be released as a single album. The rest of the material would end up as B-sides on the album's single releases, with songs such as "Spanish Eyes" and "Sweetest Thing," or included on expanded anniversary deluxe editions of *The Joshua Tree*. Several of the B-sides have become fan favorites over "Trip Through Your Wires," with even "Sweetest Thing" being re-recorded as a single in 1998, but those songs did not have the narrative direction and gritty roots quality U2 was aiming to achieve on *The Joshua Tree*. Sonically capturing that essence was integral in conveying the message they sought to communicate. It was not enough to share this message of America, but it had to sound like America as well.

In the lyrics, we encounter the scene of a broken man calling out to a woman. The man is shaking and in pain but is ultimately put back together by this woman. She clothes him and gives him shelter from the harsh elements. At this man's most desperate hour, the woman wets his lips to satiate his thirst. Now, he is caught up in his desire for this woman.

Though, as the song's narrative progresses, it is possible that this woman is not the salvation she appears to be. Bono sings in the song's chorus asking if the woman is an angel or a devil. Though, the man may not care as he was on the brink of some truly terrible experience, perhaps death, but he does wish to know the intentions this woman has for him despite his desire for her. In the final verse, Bono sings of thunder on the mountain and a rain cloud in the desert sky with the man still calling out. At the end of the song, whether the woman has saved the man from the storm or if she is the storm itself remains unclear and adds to the mystery surrounding the woman's presence.

Bono described the inspiration for the lyrics of "Trip Through Your Wires" as originating from phone calls he had with a figure that may have been acting disingenuously with him while U2 was touring America. He had felt this person was acting like someone he or she was not. [McCormick and U2, *U2 by U2*, 184] Although "Trip Through Your Wires" musically meshes with *The Joshua Tree*'s themes, Stokes says, "lyrically it's relatively throwaway." He expands on this though, suggesting,

> It can be seen as another paean to the contradictory charms of America, personified as a woman. It could be about an unconventional sexual encounter and the attendant feelings of confusion and guilt. Or it can be read simply as an exercise in personal myth-making of the kind Dylan initiates would have been more familiar with: the singer broken down by the ravages of living the hard life being put back together by the love of a good woman (or even a bad one!). [Stokes, *Into the Heart*, 74]

I find Stokes' comments on the lyrics being a throwaway to be a bit overstated. Just as the music of "Trip Through Your Wires" contributes to *The Joshua Tree*'s musical aesthetic, so do the lyrics contribute to the album's larger themes, specifically about the search for salvation. At the heart of *The Joshua Tree* is the concept of journeying and discovery, and U2 broaches this theme in multiple ways. In addition to their journey highlighting the hypocrisy of US policies, there is an exploration of the band's spirituality as well as the temptations and obstacles they encounter and overcome. Although "I Still Haven't Found What I'm Looking For" is *The Joshua Tree*'s most obvious track about searching for an answer through salvation, "Trip Through Your Wires" contributes to that concept with a narrative that is seemingly less obvious but nonetheless integral to the overall theme of the album.

Several songs on *The Joshua Tree* directly point a finger at Reagan and his administration's policies. Whether funding military interventions in foreign lands or denying its own citizens a chance at the American Dream, the concept of America's dichotomy remains strong throughout the album, and "Trip Through Your Wires" is no exception to that. Much like the narrative of "In God's Country," the story in "Trip Through Your Wires" is one of finding liberation through salvation amid an unforgiving landscape and mysterious figures with unknown intentions. As opposed to the siren calling out and beckoning one to approach in the former song, the latter plays out a scene where the salvation comes to the afflicted. Just as Bono adds a layer of caution to the Statue of Liberty's siren song in "In God's Country," the woman in "Trip Through Your Wires" may not be the rescuer she appears to be.

Based on that, it could be reasoned that the woman in the song represents America, or more specifically, American policies. Though the woman's intentions are not known to the man, it does not matter because he exhibits a need for her to survive. Though we do not know the circumstances of why the man needs saving—perhaps the source of his inflictions could be a reaction to America's dichotomy adversely affecting its own heartland citizens, as represented by the harsh desert environment—he is desperate for salvation and will take it from whoever can offer it, regardless if that perceived salvation stems from the cause of the original plight.

Thinking on this, I recall back to the last line of "Bullet the Blue Sky" when the women and children run into the arms of America, the country that wrought devastation on them in the first place. That scene is not unlike the one in "Trip Through Your Wires" when the narrative is framed as the desert representing the harshness of a dichotomous America and the woman representing a false salvation. This keeps people dependent on a system that is cyclical in its cause and treatment of a rift in American culture, which perpetuates the divide between the American Dream and the American Reality. With the way things are for the man in the song, he appears to not have a choice in the matter. He can either take the salvation offered or die.

The narrative of "Trip Through Your Wires," and to some extent "In God's Country," relies on the trope of women representing a figure or idea whose intentions could be to deceive or mislead men. In both songs, but especially more pronounced in "Trip Through Your Wires," a woman is the embodiment of temptation and salvation within the spiritual and emotional constructs of *The Joshua Tree*. The man, encountered by the woman whose intentions are unclear, is forced by his own perilous situation to give into the relief the woman is offering. Bono has commented before that he idealizes women, but the narrative of these songs reveals a level of complexity inherent in U2's existential wanderings through the American desert in *The Joshua Tree*. Not only is the man suffering in the song not aware if this woman is an angel or devil, but it also does not matter given his broken state. He needs her salvation regardless of her intentions with him. Within the broader scope of the album, it reveals facets of U2's relationship with America. Much like Bono idealizing women despite embracing gendered narrative tropes to illustrate the song's meaning, U2 also accepts the notion that to love America means to criticize and critique its flaws. Their admiration and admonition of America are not mutually exclusive. They are aware of America's systemic issues, but they give in to and embrace the allure of its more noble and brighter features as a means of witnessing and questioning its darker qualities. U2 achieving newfound fame and success was America wetting their lips, and regardless of its intentions, they still acknowledged and denounced the flaws within its inherent dichotomy. Within the scope of *The Joshua Tree*, America is both an angel and devil. To deal with one means to reckon with the other. U2's embracing of America meant that although one can accept its salvation, it cannot be at the expense of denying the same for others. "Trip Through Your Wires" acknowledges the trap America can set due to nationalist and racist policies, and the conflict that sometimes someone has to take what is offered before finding the strength to spring that trap.

During The Joshua Tree Tour 2017, Bono introduced the song by saying it was the band exploring their Irish heritage in American roots music. On the projection screen, the audience viewed a dual video presentation featuring two women, one swinging a lasso dressed in a seductive appropriation of western-style fashion with jeans, cowboy hat, and American flag bikini top, while the other painted an American flag on the side of a derelict desert shack in slow motion. What may, on the surface, appear to be a moment of blending sex appeal with forced patriotism on part of the band during this point of the concert could actually be a subtle jab at Trump's manipulation of Americans. Being that the man in "Trip Through Your Wires" is unaware of the woman's true intentions and also the song contributing to the theme of criticizing American politics, we could also be skeptical of the woman's purpose during the 2017 tour video. Depending on how it is viewed, the American flag painting and alluring western clothing could be a patriotic celebration or veiled propaganda, or given the narrative of this song as well as the one for "In God's Country," this woman could represent America as the siren.

In an interview with *Rolling Stone*, on the topic of Trump, the Edge said that things had come full circle between the Reagan era of 1980s US politics and the politics of the Trump administration. [Greene, "The Edge"] When considering the woman in "Trip Through Your Wires," in the context of both *The Joshua Tree* and the 2017 tour, no one knows if the man in the song's narrative is being manipulated or saved. There is an ambiguity that plays well into the theme of the album, which remains relevant when contextualized amid the US political climate. It all depends on how what is going on is perceived. If someone is in dire need of salvation, it may come in many forms—even one that will not really save.

CHAPTER NINE

These City Walls

U2's conceptualized exploration of America was becoming increasingly realized as they continued work on *The Joshua Tree*. They had addressed the Reagan administration's foreign policy and condemned its military intervention in foreign conflicts, explored the intersection of violence and religion occupying the minds of those struggling on the fringes of the American Dream, reconciled with their own inner demons and temptation, and found the hidden beauty within a deceitfully desolate American landscape. They had found answers and meaning, but were still left with questions. Influenced by America's musical past, U2 would recall their own history and learn the ultimate truth about what lies beyond the end of one's journey.

Just as with many of the other songs on *The Joshua Tree*, "I Still Haven't Found What I'm Looking For" originated from a jam session. This process, which U2 had historically relied on, placed the band's emphasis on achieving the sound they had desired and then adding lyrics later to complement the music. Working in this improvisational style was their preferred method as musicians who had valued their sonic qualities over songwriting ability. Bono, until the recording of *The Joshua Tree*, did not really consider words at all important within the context of rock music, citing them as old-fashioned. Though, as U2's exploration of America continued, they would find that their music, as well as songwriting, would evolve as they discovered more about American culture.

In *U2 by U2*, Adam reflected on how "I Still Haven't Found What I'm Looking For" had changed from its origin as a jam curiously titled "Under the Weather Girls," saying it was "a bit of a one-note groove, but it had a great drum part." Working on the song, a new rhythm-and-blues melody emerged and the drum part from the original jam session was kept for this early iteration of the song. Larry echoes Adam's statement by discussing the role Lanois played in the development of "I Still Haven't Found What I'm Looking For," saying that Lanois was focused on the rhythm section for the song and kept encouraging him to work on it further. Lanois' production kept the song's composition simple by ultimately removing much of the drum pattern and leaving only the song's basic melody. [McCormick and U2, *U2 by U2*, 181]

For the song, Bono wanted to explore the concept of spiritual doubt. Inspired by the use of biblical imagery by Southern American writers, Bono related to the powerful images they evoked. America's neoconservative movement championed by the Reagan administration was opening up Bono's eyes to the hypocrisies of America's dichotomy. For a country that championed itself as a promised land, America failed to live up to the commitment for all its inhabitants, leaving those marginalized on the fringes of American prosperity behind in the desert dust. The mythos of America was incredibly important to U2 growing up in Ireland, and despite the atrocities and cultural wasteland they witnessed, the ideals within that mythos were worthy of striving to secure and maintain. Although the band believed America could indeed live up to the ideals of a promised land, it sometimes became difficult for them, and especially for Bono, as doubt grew and their faith was tested.

Bono wanted to capture his spiritual doubt as part of *The Joshua Tree*'s exploration of the American dichotomy in a way that Brian Eno said that the songs Bono was advocating for contained such a level of self-conscious spirituality that it made him look not very cool. [*Classic Albums, The Joshua Tree*] For Bono to address the spiritual feelings he was struggling with, it became important for U2 to explore, and ultimately find inspiration in, American gospel music, a genre in which marginalized Black Americans sang about faith and spirituality through the lens of their people's history in the country, to give *The Joshua Tree* a distinctly American sound.

In an interview in *Classic Albums*, Lanois reflected on introducing gospel music to U2 and the role it played in the recording of "I Still Haven't Found What I'm Looking For" by suggesting that he had always admired gospel music, which he would then encourage the band to explore, completely aware that it had not been a typical genre for U2 to explore given their previous albums rooted in punk. Lanois believed that gospel music would expand their horizons, motivating the band to experiment with sounds and sonic landscapes previously unknown and unfamiliar to them. During recording, he felt the band was pushing themselves to achieve this new musical quality, including Bono singing at the peak of his vocal range. For Lanois, this feeling was palpable and he said it was almost like hearing Aretha Franklin, a sign that U2 could deliver a gospel element in their music. [*Classic Albums, The Joshua Tree*]

Though gospel, with artists such as the Staple Singers, was a source of inspiration on a musical level for U2 while recording *The Joshua Tree*, the genre's inclusion of political and social messaging through the lens of faith and spirituality was important to the band's development at this time as well. During the US civil rights movement, Black musicians recorded spiritual anthems such as "Go Tell It on the Mountain" and "We Shall Overcome," or even more obscure songs such as "Give Me Liberty or Give Me Death," as B-sides to their more popular and perceived radio friendly singles. The purpose, according to Robert Darden, the founder of Baylor University's Black Gospel Music Restoration Project, was to hide protest songs in plain sight without fear of punishment or retribution. Darden explains that Black Americans had limited options to share their voice so spirituals, gospel music, and devotionals became a way for these performers to convey their feelings safely. [PRI and WNYC, "Rediscovering"]

To commemorate the 50th anniversary of the University of California, Berkeley's Free Speech Movement, several musicians and activists gathered to discuss the role of music as protest and as a driver of the civil rights movement. Kim Nalley, a jazz and blues vocalist, criticized the role rock music has in contemporary society, suggesting that rock performers, who are predominantly white, are unaware of the roots of their music and where it comes from. Modern rock music, according to Nalley, came from the evolution of spirituals that, when the music entered the church, became gospel and soul music. These evolved forms of music gave a voice to the civil rights and freedom movements that then continued into rock music. [Gilbert, "Singing It Right Out Loud"]

Given the historical context in which gospel music played a role during the civil rights movement and advancing the rights of Black Americans, it might have been unconvincing two decades after the movement what four white men from Ireland intended to do with the tradition. Bono recalled that it became a challenge when recording "I Still Haven't Found What I'm Looking For" to channel the spirit of an old gospel song into a contemporary setting without losing its essence while also having respect for its history. [*Classic Albums, The Joshua Tree*] For U2, that meant honoring the tradition of gospel but adding their own cultural perspective as outsiders to comment on the disillusionment of faith and spiritual doubt that they experienced during their existential journey through America.

The lyrics for "I Still Haven't Found What I'm Looking For" are about the pilgrimage one undertakes to seek a destination whether it be an eternal truth, salvation, or some other divine reward. Bono's appreciation of the legacy of gospel music, as well as Southern American writers and their use of biblical imagery, certainly shines through in the song as he sings about climbing high mountains and running through fields to be with the reward of his journey he seeks. He recounts all the trials, scaling city walls and walking the fine line between angels and devils, he had to overcome to achieve that spiritual release. Though, through it all, he has yet to find deliverance and must continue the journey. What he has been looking for has yet to be found.

There is much hope, despite his spiritual doubt and struggles, in finding the salvation Bono is seeking in the song. He knows, on a level that only faith can ascribe, that there is a Kingdom Come where all the colors combine into one, suggesting the power of a great equalizer that sheds humanity of the artifice that furthers its own divisions. These distractions of mankind will not stop him, so he still keeps running and searching. Motivated by the salvation he seeks to break his bonds, loosen his chains, and carry the cross of his shame, Bono pushes forward to find the salvation that would validate his faith and remove his doubts. Greg Garrett, in his book *We Get to Carry Each Other: The Gospel According to U2*, says the significance of the lesson in "I Still Haven't Found What I'm Looking For" is that "life is a journey, not a destination; faith is a means, not an end. It's okay to go on looking, especially if you've got the sense you know which direction you're travelling." [Garrett, *We Get to Carry*, 117] Bono would suggest that the song does not affirm anything in the way that previous gospel and spiritual music that inspired him did, but it did share with them elements of pure joy and a restless spirit. [Turner, *Imagine*]

When considering Garrett's analysis of the song's gospel messaging, as well as Bono's comments about the song not being within the ordinary gospel tradition, the role of "I Still Haven't Found What I'm Looking For," within the context of *The Joshua Tree*, continues the political legacy of the gospel anthems of the civil rights movement that inspired it. Bono is not only searching for his own spiritual salvation in the song but also the salvation of all people. Within *The Joshua Tree*, the song speaks truth to power to America's leaders and their fundamentalist supporters to work toward making America a promised land for all people instead of just the wealthy elite or those who practice a particular faith, a place where all colors bleed into one.

On this journey, U2 were witnessing the hypocrisy of US policies that contributed to the widening division of its people, oppressing those who are marginalized by class, religion, or race, destining them to be cast out to exist on the fringes of the American Dream. Although activists and civil rights leaders did make progress in their fight for freedoms, and still do, there is still a long way to go toward achieving the American Dream for all Americans. This is reflected in the journey Bono goes through in "I Still Haven't Found What I'm Looking For." The journey is arduous and what is sought may never be found, but the prospect of achieving equality for all of humanity is what continues the motivation to push forward and keep searching. It is the belief in this idea of freedom from oppression that drives one to take the first steps on the journey toward turning a dream into reality.

The lyrics of "I Still Haven't Found What I'm Looking For" also uphold the larger themes of *The Joshua Tree* with respect to overcoming temptation and aligning one's self with a moral rightness that embodies U2's idealized vision of America. In his essay "Fallen Angels in the Hands of U2" in *Exploring U2*, Deane Galbraith says that the song's lyrics suggests that "the moral choices that Bono has made throughout his life are alternately aligned with the ranks of benign or evil angels" and that his lyrics "are filled with allusions to an invisible cosmic dimension existing beyond earthly ethical and external struggles." [Galbraith, "Fallen Angels," 184] Galbraith's comments on "I Still Haven't Found What I'm Looking For" echoes the narratives of other songs from the album as well. We see U2 grappling with their own morality and ethics throughout *The Joshua Tree* with songs such as "Exit" exploring murderous intentions borne from fringe isolationism, succumbing to vice and sin in "Running to Stand Still," the drive for salvation via temptation in "Trip Through Your Wires," as well as the moralistic outrage expressed in "Bullet the Blue Sky" and "Mothers of the Disappeared." Expanded to reflect the entirety of *The Joshua Tree*, we see how Galbraith's comments can illustrate the album's complete narrative. This existential journey through America is fraught with temptation and peril, but there is a larger force guiding U2. "I Still Haven't Found What I'm Looking For" is representative of the idea that despite the problems with America, and the many ways it can overtake someone, there is something far greater to strive toward and that America can represent an extension of God's love in the form of eliminating its destructive nationalist and racist policies—an act that requires facing and standing up against the nation's inherent evils as a means of finding what U2 is looking for in the image of America they seek to uphold.

In much of *The Joshua Tree*, such as with "Bullet the Blue Sky," U2 is critical about the hypocrisy of fundamentalist Christianity and its influence on American culture. In *Walk On: The Spiritual Journey of U2*, Steve Stockman documents U2's spiritual path from the band's early days and details how religion played a fluctuating role in their career. While U2 have been described at times as Christian torchbearers, Stockman states that "I Still Haven't Found What I'm Looking For" was a "pivotal song in the band's artistic intentions and spiritual development." Stockman suggests that the song dismissed a fundamentalist belief that "Jesus is the answer" and that "there is nothing left to search for" with U2 instead espousing that "following Jesus is a journey, not an arrival." [Stockman, *Walk On*, 71–72]

Stockman suggests that this approach to their spiritual thinking allowed U2 to get closer to the truth. In contrast with the belief of Christian fundamentalists, some who had followed the band since their early days believing them to be an outwardly and unwavering

Christian rock band, Stockman says that "'I Still Haven't Found What I'm Looking For' is an indication that U2 might have been closer to biblical truth than the narrow and precise Christians that pointed their finger." [Stockman, *Walk On*, 73] Within the overall context of *The Joshua Tree*, the band's exploration, understanding, and expression of their faith as a journey reflects the album's narrative and the gospel influences that motivated U2 to critique America. America living up to its idealized pronouncements of being a promised land becomes the journey not only at the heart of "I Still Haven't Found What I'm Looking For" but also with *The Joshua Tree* as a whole.

As part of their existential exploration of America, U2 had seen just how much neoconservative fundamentalist Christian influence in US politics devastated the well-being of Americans as well as people elsewhere. With televangelists like Jerry Falwell, who had Reagan's ear and could help direct policy, there was a need for U2 to call out the hypocrisies of them espousing Christian doctrine while being driven by greed and white supremacy. Bono feels modern Christian fundamentalism poses an extreme threat and is dangerous. He knows the good guys win in the end of the biblical story, but the nefarious forces guiding fundamentalism turn religion into an industry. Bono equates this fundamentalist impact on Christianity to McDonald's to express the movement being devoid of the ideology's true value, evoking the fast food chain to suggest fundamentalism is lacking in real spiritual sustenance. [Black, *Bono in His Own Words*, 31]

Relying on the spiritual influence of gospel music, U2 crafted "I Still Haven't Found What I'm Looking For" as a spiritual anthem for the new age. One that dismissed the notion of a perfect faith but rather espoused the benefits of the journey as something that can be achieved if we consider the needs of everyone over the needs of the few. For in the journey, there is wisdom, introspection, and a resistance to the notion that salvation is something that represents a singular vision. The Edge recalled his spiritual development during recording *The Joshua Tree*, saying that although none of his core beliefs had changed when recording the album, they had grown in relation to his own experiences, which consisted of an understanding about what is good within the world and the toxic elements of religion throughout. In understanding that there is no perfect expression of spirituality, the Edge believed he matured in his understanding while recording the album. [*Hot Press*, "The Edge Goes Solo"]

During recording of "I Still Haven't Found What I'm Looking For," with Adam and Larry working on the rhythm section, the Edge went to work crafting the song's melody. In the early stages, the Edge heard the rhythm section and described it as like "'Eye of the Tiger' played by a reggae band." The band continued working on the song and, with the help of Lanois and Mark "Flood" Ellis mixing, the song came together in a way the Edge would describe as "full-on electricity-in-the-air creativity." [McCormick and U2, *U2 by U2*, 181]

As Bono was singing the lyrics, the Edge remembered he had written down a potential title for the song. Listening to Bono's singing, the Edge noticed that a rich soulful melody was forming and that the song title he had written down could be a good fit and handed Bono the paper with the song title as he was singing. He further realized that the elements coming together were creating one of the best songs of *The Joshua Tree* recording sessions and often played it for friends and staff from Island Records. [McCormick and U2, *U2 by U2*, 181]

Since its release as the second single from *The Joshua Tree* during May 1987, "I Still Haven't Found What I'm Looking For" has become one of U2's most beloved songs. It hit number one on the US Billboard Hot 100 chart, became a staple during their live performances, and has garnered critical recognition, appearing in multiple publications as one of the greatest songs of all time. Beyond the critical and commercial success of the single, "I Still Haven't Found What I'm Looking For" established that U2 had effectively captured much of their existential American journey on *The Joshua Tree*. Their discovery and exploration of American culture through its music, spirituality, and politics, with the release of "I Still Haven't Found What I'm Looking For," resulted in U2 achieving exactly what they set out to accomplish: a culmination of their examination of the complexities of the American dichotomy and a declaration of their belief that the country's divisions could be bridged with a common goal that protects all people.

Although the recording of "I Still Haven't Found What I'm Looking For" in 1986 contained an inherent commentary on America's neoconservative and fundamentalist movements, the journeying spirit of the song remains relevant today amid the current political climate. In support of The Joshua Tree Tour 2017, U2 performed the song on *Jimmy Kimmel Live*. Introducing it as a gospel song with a restless spirit, U2 performed it with a backing choir planted among members of the audience. [Kimmel, interview]

Most notable from this appearance on *Jimmy Kimmel Live* was how U2 modernized the messaging of the song's context. Though written at a time when Bono was filled with doubt and contempt over televangelist Christians, during the interview with Kimmel, Bono took a moment to condemn the terrorist bombing of an Ariana Grande concert that occurred in Manchester, England, the night before. Commenting on the fundamentalist Islamic terrorist attack, Bono said that the attack in Manchester represented the darker aspect of what humanity has to offer. However, as a response to the outpouring of humanitarianism that occurred in its aftermath, Bono's faith held firm when he saw citizens responding to the attacks by sheltering victims in their homes and lining up to donate blood, signifying a spirit that cannot be broken by extremism and fundamentalism. [Kimmel, interview]

In the United States, the undefeatable spirit of humanity Bono believes in continues to push the nation in a direction that embodies the spirit of a promised land it has been historically heralded to be. Since the advent of Black Lives Matter and other racial justice groups in recent years, protesting against the unconscionable murder of Black lives such as George Floyd at the hands and knees of police, America continues to reconcile with the sins of the nation's forefathers and their modern iterations. New waves of protests demanding racial and social justice, guided by their movements' leaders and artists, directly challenge the culture of division Trump advanced as he pushed an agenda that emboldened white supremacy under the guise of law and order, a dog-whistle attempt to further expand the widening divide in the country. More than three decades later, "I Still Haven't Found What I'm Looking For" still shines as an optimistic anthem for the country's restless spirit impacted by Trump's administration, compelling listeners to reflect on the best of humanity as a means of resisting against its worst elements as part of a collective journey toward something far greater.

During The Joshua Tree Tour 2017, the band performed "I Still Haven't Found What I'm Looking For" in a celebratory way that relished the experience of playing one of their most admired songs for crowds that could sing along with every word. With black-and-white video of desert fauna appearing on the giant projection screen, the song, within that context, was an ode to the landscape imagery and gospel music that influenced the band three decades prior. "I Still Haven't Found What I'm Looking For" is a song about the hope and doubt experienced during life's journey, and The Joshua Tree Tour 2017 performances reflected that with a jubilant flourish. However, at the heart of celebration, the song also represents that we have an ongoing responsibility to resist oppression and fundamentalism in all of its forms, whether they be from a terrorist attack, police violence, or a presidential policy.

CHAPTER TEN

Sweet the Sin

ALTHOUGH *THE JOSHUA TREE* IS AN ALBUM THAT REFLECTS U2'S EXIS-
tential journey through America and discovering its inherent dichotomy, part of that journey included the band understanding their own
Irishness in relation, and not every song on the album directly addresses
a distinctly American issue. Adding homegrown emotional depth to
the album, the band drew parallels between struggles they witnessed
in America with what they had witnessed, and could potentially have
experienced, in Ireland. During the journey of recording *The Joshua Tree*,
U2 would come to find that temptation, often an obstacle or catalyst in
the search of salvation, was a force that dominated all of humanity.

Drug abuse was a topic U2 had dealt with before on their previous
album *The Unforgettable Fire* from 1984. "Wire," the third track on
the album, was a song about Bono commenting on Dublin's growing
heroin epidemic in the early 1980s, which included him knowing some
friends who used it and were addicted, with the song's lyrics expressing
ambivalence to it. In "Wire," there is an acerbic tone as Bono sings lines
saying the subject in the song's narrative feels like today is a nice day to
throw his or her life away. Despite a perceived air of judgment, Bono
recognized that he too, having grown up and still living in Dublin at the
time, could have shared the same fate as others he knew and suggested

that he perhaps suffers from an addictive personality himself. [*Hot Press*, "I Still Haven't Found"]

The other song on *The Unforgettable Fire* to address drug abuse, and the one performed during Live Aid that catapulted U2 to success, was "Bad." Originating from a tune improvised by the Edge, "Bad" is a considerably more compassionate track than "Wire" as Bono continues to struggle with an internal conflict regarding drug abuse and his own temptation. In *Into the Heart*, Niall Stokes says, "There is a sense throughout 'Bad' that [Bono] doesn't know what he wants to say, and that he doesn't know what he's saying either. But, in a way, he says it eloquently." [Stokes, *Into the Heart*, 58] That eloquence Bono puts into the track comes from a realization that he could fall easily to temptation just like anyone else can. He even sings in the song that he would let go and surrender if he could.

As U2 were becoming more successful as a band, their opportunities for the excess of a rock-and-roll lifestyle grew. With songs like "Wire" and "Bad," Bono could have potentially been reacting to the darker allures of that lifestyle, but they also came from a deeply personal place, physically and emotionally, that U2 grew up with.

In his book *The World and U2: One Band's Remaking of Global Activism*, Alan McPherson discusses the level of poverty Ireland faced and U2's exposure to it at an early age. McPherson describes Bono's and the Edge's upbringing as being middle-class, compared to Larry's and Adam's families being working class. [McPherson, *The World and U2*, 4] He cites Bono recalling his childhood home on Cedarwood Road being a "nice street with nice families. People who shaped my world view. People I still love and admire." [U2, *Songs of Innocence* liner notes]

Adjacent to the neighborhood where Bono would grow up was Ballymun Flats, a building complex of seven residential towers built in 1967 to relocate Dublin's slum residents to rejuvenate the city's infrastructure. Adversely, this block of residential buildings, according to

McPherson, resulted in environmental and social damage describing, with Dublin's poor and disenfranchised now clustered together, "out of poverty came violence." [McPherson, *The World and U2*, 4]

Ballymun Flats were designed to modernize Ireland by building an infrastructure that supported high-rise communities. In *U2 by U2*, Bono noted that Ireland had begun construction on these residential towers after the rest of Europe had already realized that such community developments only exacerbated the problems they sought to resolve. He recalled playing in the foundations of the buildings while they were under construction and when they were completed, including riding the elevators up and down until they fell into disrepair due to poor maintenance and the building began reeking of stale urine. [McCormick and U2, *U2 by U2*, 182]

Dublin, though only 60 miles away from the border of Northern Ireland, the center of sectarian violence during the three decade long conflict known as the Troubles, generally saw much less violence than in the north and instead was plagued by its own problems. As a result, in *Race of Angels: The Genesis of U2*, Irish columnist and author John Waters claimed that U2 and others were part of a "generation of young Irish people which had its own experience of being isolated behind the lines of a war in which it was not involved." [Waters, *Race of Angels*, 33] With no war or terroristic violence in the streets of Dublin near the frequent and devastating scale of that within the north plagued by those living in the heart of the Troubles, McPherson and Waters assert that U2 were largely unaffected by the violence in Northern Ireland, with Bono being relatively removed and the Edge suggesting the effect within their community was not direct. [McPherson, *The World and U2*, 4] Without the distractions of bombings or sectarian murders, the marginalized citizens of Dublin could destroy themselves in solitude within the walls of building complexes like Ballymun Flats, a modernized symbol of Ireland's status as one of the poorest countries in western Europe at that time.

Dublin's city government, as part of its modernization efforts, demolished the slums and displaced its residents into high-rises like Ballymun Flats. As a result, friends and neighbors who had built strong relationships and identities within their communities often lost touch with each other after relocating to the high-rises. Often removed and isolated from their former communities as well as any opportunities to modernize and progress alongside more middle-class communities, the conditions and infrastructure of their new homes further complicated the issues of its lower-class inhabitants. Bono recalled that issues the poorer residents faced while living in the slums often were exacerbated as they became crammed alongside the other dysfunctional lives concentrated within these buildings. [McCormick and U2, *U2 by U2*, 182]

When recording *The Joshua Tree*, Ballymun Flats and the stories U2 would hear about heroin abuse became the basis for the song "Running to Stand Still." Unlike the judgmental tone of "Wire," U2 would conceptually return to and expand upon the compassion and vulnerability of "Bad" to shed a light, musically and thematically, on Ireland's heroin epidemic, which had grown considerably during the 1980s, with this song. Noting that Bono personalized his experiences with Ballymun Flats to address Dublin's heroin epidemic, Adam described "Running to Stand Still" as a sequel to "Bad." [McCormick and U2, *U2 by U2*, 182]

The subject matter of "Running to Stand Still" was deeply personal to U2 and their connection to it was evident during its recording. In *U2 by U2*, the Edge noted that "Running to Stand Still" originated during the sessions fully formed and realized, which was unusual considering the difficulty they experienced with some songs from *The Joshua Tree* sessions. Reflecting on the session for the song, the Edge said he was idly waiting to play piano for another track when he began playing a few chords. After Lanois started to play alongside the Edge with his guitar, the rest of the band joined in. As is often the case when U2 recorded in the studio, "Running to Stand Still" was born out of improvisation. The Edge recalled that the initial playthrough of the song had all of the key components of a song, already containing a spirit and character that quickly came together after a few more takes. [McCormick and U2, *U2 by U2*, 182]

Musically, "Running to Stand Still" is one of the most fascinating tracks on *The Joshua Tree*. Not pieced together with the same production precision and wizardry as with some other songs on the album, its musical beauty lies within the ease of its flow and looseness. The Edge on piano, playing D and G chords, conveys an elegant feeling of transcendence over Larry's quiet drums, Lanois' rhythm guitar, Adam's subdued bass, and Bono's melancholic vocals and harmonica. Lanois recalled that "Running to Stand Still" was a song that brought the whole group together, bonded by the energy and communication in the studio. Lanois felt that this spirit is captured on *The Joshua Tree* because it was recorded with a presence of performance. [O'Hare, "The Secret History"]

In addition to the historical and social elements that contributed to the song's composition, the music of "Running to Stand Still" is also notable for the thematic imagery it conjures within its narrative. While it was based on a real place in Dublin and reflected the real problems many people suffered, the song is arranged to contain influences from traditional American folk and roots music, a quality U2 wanted to maintain as part of their exploration of America. The song opens with an acoustic slide guitar that reflected the band's recent fascination with American blues and country music as well as both Eno's and Lanois' appreciation of the genres that is inherent throughout the album's production. By giving a distinctly American sound to Ireland's drug epidemic, "Running to Stand Still" recognizes that the problem of isolating poverty-stricken and marginalized groups is broader than U2's own personal experiences growing up in Ireland. Although U2 were largely unexposed to problems beyond the city limits of Dublin during the

1960s and 1970s as children, their existential journey through America while recording *The Joshua Tree* opened their eyes to the reality that there exist places like Ballymun Flats all over the world, from housing projects in large cities to ramshackle hovels in desert towns. During this journey, U2 witnessed these isolated communities in the towns and deserts across America and wrote about them for songs like "In God's Country," but "Running to Stand Still" thematically connects the struggles of those stricken with poverty in Ireland with America as part of U2's vision for *The Joshua Tree*.

Just like the music, Bono's lyrics for "Running to Stand Still" were written from a fully formed narrative inspired by his own experiences with Ballymun Flats as well as a story about a couple he had heard about who lived there and were both heroin addicts. The male partner would support their habit by running drugs through Amsterdam and smuggling them back to Ireland. The strength of their addiction was understood by Bono because of his acknowledgment of the relationship between risk and reward, risking a decade-long jail sentence to continue indulging in their addiction. [McCormick and U2, *U2 by U2*, 182]

Within the bleakness of the song's narrative of drug abuse and helplessness, the story Bono tells in "Running to Stand Still" contains a desperate glimmer of hope and salvation, albeit a rather dim one that it is almost a hallucination. The narrative, written from a woman's perspective, opens with her waking up from a drug-induced sleep and, while coming down from the high, starts to reflect on her life and the need to break away from her crippling addiction. She describes the existence as a darkness in the night, with darkness symbolizing a pure and creeping hold heroin has on her which seeks to swallow her up within its blackness. She yearns for some means of deliverance through escape from her addiction with Bono describing her plight as seeking shelter from the driving rain.

Though she has an underlying urge to break free from this addiction, she is grounded by the reality of her situation. She sees seven towers, the song's reference to Ballymun Flats, but there is only one way out: a defeated realization that the only true escape from her existence is through heroin. With that escape, she feels the sweetness of heroin's sin despite the bitter taste in her mouth, which serves as a metaphor for the drug's effect on her body and mind. The imagery of her escaping the driving rain, born from this resignation that heroin is her only attainable option, implies an internal conflict that reveals several meanings regarding her relationship to the drug as being central to the idea of escape: her desire to escape from the storm that is heroin abuse that surrounds her and that Ballymun Flats is the refuge from the storm where she can drift away through heroin as an escape from the harshness of her reality.

Bono's next lines further explore this internal conflict, the effects of which reveal the contradictions of feeling normal through drug abuse within the woman when she takes heroin. He illustrates this by singing that the woman's life exists within paradoxes such as crying without weeping and being unable to scream without raising her voice. These lines, and their paradoxical expression of struggling with the conflict of addiction, stem from a conversation Bono had with his brother. Bono recalled that his brother was going through a difficult period with his business and that the experience of keeping it going was "like running to stand still." Bono had been unfamiliar with the phrase and felt it fit the experience of people struggling with heroin addiction. [McCormick and U2, *U2 by U2*, 182]

The phrase "running to stand still," which is used only as the closing line of the song, perfectly encapsulates the woman's, as well as many addicts', experiences. Bono is able to tenderly reveal an addict's need to find normalcy and express and resolve the conflicts within themselves. The woman wants to break free from this life but does not have the means to do so. There is a desperate plea in the struggle that is drowned out by resignation. Preceding the final line, the song reveals that the woman will succumb to the chilly lure and temptation of the needle. Although the escape the woman ultimately yearns for involves breaking the chains that bind her to the seven towers, she succumbs to the illusion of escape through her addiction, thus committing herself to her addiction that is aggravated and worsened by social and economic forces beyond her control.

Bono illustrates the woman giving in to her addiction as her drinking from a poison stream and floating out of her reality. Within this scene, the song's narrative point of view changes from the woman to someone who is witnessing her descent into addiction, potentially another person or the woman having an out of body experience as a representation of disassociation through heroin use. Either way, this perspective sees the woman walking through streets in the driving rain with bloodshot eyes. The woman approaches this person bringing white golden pearls that were stolen from the sea, representing either heroin itself or some realization found within the realm of this drug-induced escapism. This person looks into the woman's eyes and sees a raging storm within them, signifying that the drug is not the relief it is believed to be but an extension of the torment of her reality that infiltrates her escapism.

Although the woman is the narrative center of the song, it is the other person in the scenario that offers many possibilities for interpretation regarding their role and the significance of their presence. If this person is not representative of the woman's heroin-induced disassociation and is actually an observer to the woman's struggles, they could be the husband Bono had heard about. Bono felt the husband in the story was a decent person despite his addictions and acknowledged that his wife was at the back of his mind when writing "Running to Stand Still," [McCormick and U2, *U2 by U2*, 182] but that would not adequately elucidate the drama of the situation and the importance of seeing the storm in the woman's eyes. More likely, given the narrative threads within *The Joshua Tree* concerning temptation, the other person in the song could be Bono, and his appearance demonstrates the vulnerability and allure associated with heroin previously expressed in "Bad."

Despite being major rock stars, the members of U2 have not been associated with the typical rock star trope of abusing drugs beyond cigarette and alcohol use (with the exception of Adam being arrested for marijuana possession in 1989). In an article by Anthony DeCurtis for *Rolling Stone*, Bono described U2 as being a freak show. He felt that they were such fish out of water that they questioned what they were even doing being rock stars. He joked that U2 should have made people feel more at home by doing drugs out of guilt. [DeCurtis, "U2"]

However, Bono has been cagey regarding questions concerning him possibly dabbling with drugs. In *U2: The Definitive Biography*, Jobling notes that Bono dodging the issue, though writing about the topic for songs like "Wire" and "Bad," frustrated U2's fans and critics. [Jobling, *U2*, 210] In an interview between Bono and Adam Block, a contributor for *Mother Jones*, Block asks Bono about any previous drug use, to which Bono replied,

I don't want to talk about that. I'll give you just one example of why it would be irresponsible for me to answer your question in a certain way: I've written so many songs using heroin as an image, it might be interesting for me to tell you that, say, "I've had experiences with the drug heroin." It might be interesting for me to do it, and to own up to it. If it were misconstrued, somebody who, for whatever reason, respects me, that might lead them to get into it. OK. If I became addicted to heroin, I can afford the trappings. I can afford the Betty Ford clinic. I can afford to have my blood changed. I can afford the trappings of being an addict. But there is some guy who lives in a room in Dublin who can't. And nobody gives a shit about his addiction! [Block, "Bono Bites Back"]

Bono has been consistent with this approach when pressed on drug use. While making a point about Paul McCartney admitting to using cocaine and heroin, Michka Assayas, in his book of conversations with Bono, pressed him on his habit of shying away from directly answering questions about hard drugs while being forthright about his abuse of alcohol, to which Bono replied:

[A drunken episode] does not make headlines for an Irish person. Bottom line: I think drugs are dumb. Bottom line: I think abuse of alcohol is dumb. Bottom line: I think that cigarette smoking is dumb. And that's it, really. My point about alcohol is that if you abuse something, it abuses you back. That's really it. Whether it's a spliff, whether it's anything, there's a boomerang to it. [Assayas, *Bono*, 156]

Bono's avoidance and reluctance in not directly answering if he had ever used, or even abused, hard drugs can be traced back to the vulnerability he expressed when writing songs like "Wire" and "Bad," or with even potentially inserting himself in "Running to Stand Still" where he would come face to face with heroin addiction within the track's narrative. There is a fear there coupled with a tenderness that Bono has always related to. Not only did he grow up near Ballymun Flats, but he also personally knew people who battled, or even lost the fight, against heroin. Bono's longtime friend, the avant-garde artist Guggi, a member of The Virgin Prunes, lived at Ballymun Flats for several years and Phil Lynott, lead vocalist and bassist for Thin Lizzy as well as Bono's neighbor at one point, died in 1986 as a result of complications and issues stemming from his heroin addiction. [McCormick and U2, *U2 by U2*, 182] All of these people came from the same background and lived in the same area. They were all susceptible to the same allure of heroin, a curse within Dublin that could have potentially tempted and threatened Bono.

In an interview with *Hot Press*, Bono expressed that he did not necessarily lack sympathy for those who use drugs because he understood the appeal. He had understood it growing up and, as a rock star, his understanding of the allure deepened. [Stokes, "The World About Us"] Though Bono suggested he has always understood the attraction to drugs, his relationship to the subject in his songwriting matured. The condemnation of throwing everything away in "Wire" evolved to wrestling with desire in "Bad." With "Running to Stand Still," Bono revealed the conditions that would compel one to toe the edge above oblivion, visualizing a scene, and perhaps narratively involving himself, at a site representing Dublin's heroin epidemic and confronting the temptation eye to eye. It is not clear if the person in the song takes the white golden pearls from the woman after staring at the storm in her eyes. Given Bono's own guarded personal history when it comes to drug abuse, "Running to Stand Still" closing on this ambiguity adds a dramatic heft that heightens the emotional struggle at the heart of the song: whether to give in to temptation, especially one with such a deeply rooted personal connection.

During The Joshua Tree tour, and even as late as the Zoo TV tour in the early 1990s, Bono would mime sticking a needle in his arm as he delivered the final line of "Running to Stand Still" to dramatically visualize the song's connection to heroin abuse. After not being included on the PopMart tour in the late 1990s and only performed during one night of the Elevation tour in 2001, "Running to Stand Still" returned in 2005 for the Vertigo tour in which the band reimagined the song's original meaning. Jobling illustrated the evolving nature of the song in a live setting, saying Bono turned "the somber junkie tale" to an "anti-persecution paean," juxtaposing a reflection of Dublin's heroin epidemic with a broader idealization about humanity overcoming national and global atrocities. [Jobling, *U2*, 305]

In her essay "Time to Heal, 'Desire' Time," Robyn Brothers analyzes the spirituality of U2's music through the lens of philosophers Gilles Deleuze and Félix Guattari's "philosophy of desire . . . in order to illuminate U2's distinctly Christian conceptualization of desire as a force of the Holy Spirit." [Brothers, "Time to Heal," 238] Just like on *The Joshua Tree*, "Running to Stand Still" followed "Bullet the Blue Sky" in concert to draw parallels between the latter's criticism of whatever military conflict America was currently engaged in, an example being US involvement in the Iraq War during the mid-2000s when the Vertigo tour was being held, with the former's narrative of "misplaced desire for transcendence through the use of heroin." Brothers suggests that U2's faith, within the scope of Deleuze's and Guattari's philosophy, results in the live performance of "Running to Stand Still" signifying that faith is a "desiring, affirming, and 'deterritorializing' force." [Brothers, "Time to Heal," 260] Brothers' analysis widens U2's inherent messaging within *The Joshua Tree* to include the power of faith as a means of addressing the individual and collective social wrongs as part of U2's critique of America, with "Running to Stand Still" representing the idea that the absolution of the sins of America comes from not persecuting those most adversely affected by its inability to be the promised land it proclaims to be. Both on the album and in a live setting, there is a search for salvation in "Running to Stand Still" that aims to bring a relief from the violence and distress of "Bullet the Blue Sky," rescuing the promised land ideals of America from annihilation at the behest of the country's own disastrous policies.

During The Joshua Tree Tour 2017, "Running to Stand Still" returned to the set list for the first time since the Vertigo tour more than a decade prior, still serving the purpose of seeking salvation from the violence of "Bullet the Blue Sky" and finding a light amid the darkness.

Although Bono often introduced songs from *The Joshua Tree* during this tour with thoughts and comments regarding their relevance in a modern context, that did not happen with "Running to Stand Still" on this tour. The responsibility of criticizing Trump's policies, especially those that stoke racism and bigotry that further divide the nation, would be executed during "Bullet the Blue Sky," which made clear that Trump's authoritarian agenda was an extremist version of the song's original critique of Reagan. Instead, the band quietly segued into "Running to Stand Still" to soothe the anxiety the audience, and much of the world, felt about the dangers of Trump's administration. In a time that America was facing an existential crisis under Trump that further expanded the gap of its own dichotomy, "Running to Stand Still" offers comfort in our ongoing need to find deliverance from the harm Trump's persecution instilled in all of us. With this song and its quiet meditation of seeking salvation, we can clear our minds of what is troubling us and focus on the search for our own deliverance.

CHAPTER ELEVEN

Scorch the Earth

THE JOSHUA TREE, OUTSIDE OF ITS POLITICAL THEMES, ALSO EXPRESSED U2's journey toward self-discovery. Through their exploration of America's musical traditions and culture, they would find the inspiration to grow on artistic and personal levels. If they were going to effectively express the American dichotomy they came to understand during this journey, they had to reevaluate how they approached their music and learn from their past. Growth, and being confident in their journey, would be essential in crafting their creative breakthrough. Recognizing civil and social unrest closer to home would give U2 a broader understanding of the economic turmoil many Americans faced in Reagan's America.

Coal mining in the United Kingdom was a nationalized industry that was proving to be unprofitable by the early 1980s. In an effort to revitalize the industry, Prime Minister Margaret Thatcher aimed to close the mines, crack down on unions, and privatize the coal mining industry. In 1984, the National Coal Board, supported and directed by Thatcher through her appointment of Ian MacGregor as the NCB's head in 1983, announced a plan that was projected to close 20 coal pits, which would then result in the loss of more than 20,000 jobs. Regional and local strikes were organized to protest the closures, which resulted in a national strike led by the National Union of Mineworkers in March 1984. This union action against Thatcher's stated goals, which was technically illegal and was deemed mob rule with Thatcher referring to the striking miners as "the enemy within." [Travis, "Thatcher"]

Over the course of a year, as the strike continued, tensions between factions within the strike and trade unions, who disapproved of the strike for not achieving a vote approving of a strike on the national level, would escalate to violence. Striking miners were pitted against strikebreakers and violent action would ensue resulting in brutal clashes with each other as well as riots with police. After nearly a year, as striking workers were struggling to put food on the table, a stalemate was reached and the workers voted to end the strike with the National Union of Mineworkers voting in favor of returning to work after failing to get enough support from other regional unions. Considered "the most bitter industrial dispute in British history" by the BBC, the yearlong strike resulted in multiple violent demonstrations, financial hardships, and even the deaths of six people. [BBC, "1984"]

During the era of the strikes, U2 released *The Unforgettable Fire* and now were looking for a new musical direction. Ireland's music scene, which at this time included groups like The Waterboys and Hothouse Flowers, was undergoing a movement that saw the resurgence of traditional Irish folk music, but adopting some of the musical and lyrical traditions of American folk and roots music. U2 had never categorically considered themselves a rock-and-roll band, so this new pursuit relying on American blues, folk, and roots music as influences served as a means of connecting their distinct style with rooted American musical traditions that were alien to them. U2's focus was trying to take a foundational element of early American rock music and infusing it with a new kind of musical spirit that the band was attempting to create in the studio. Adam described this process as attempting to revisit the basics of rock music, but the basics they were revisiting were of a different culture and background than their own. [McCormick and U2, *U2 by U2*, 172]

During this time, the transitional period often left U2 feeling creatively stalled. Prior to writing and recording *The Joshua Tree*, some members were not that familiar with traditional American roots music. In *U2 by U2*, the Edge admitted to being initially dismissive about the genre because he was only familiar with the white artists who performed adulterated appropriations of roots music after hearing them on FM radio stations during the 1970s. He described discovering public radio in the United States while touring in support of *The Unforgettable Fire* as being the turning point for him. Hearing American roots, country, and rhythm-and-blues music from genre pioneers, like Robert Johnson and Lefty Frizzell, motivated him to revisit the music as a creative direction for *The Joshua Tree*. [McCormick and U2, *U2 by U2*, 172]

U2 were absolutely focused on conveying a distinctly American feel for their next album and started working on these songs in 1985 at Larry's home in north Dublin. Several of the songs that would end up on *The Joshua Tree* originated during these jam sessions such as "Trip Through Your Wires," with its rough-and-tumble barroom blues motif. While Irish musicians at that time like The Waterboys and Hothouse Flowers were still relying heavily on traditional Irish musical traditions, U2 wanted a fresh stimulus that challenged them to take a bold direction opposite of their homeland contemporaries. Bono often dismissed what then passed as a modernized reflection of traditional Irish folk music as being watered down. [McCormick and U2, *U2 by U2*, 172] For U2, and specifically Bono, moving forward meant looking back to the past through examining the roots and foundation of the music they were being inspired by, a focused theme that would remain consistent throughout recording *The Joshua Tree*.

Though the early jam sessions at Larry's home gave some indication of U2's new American-inspired musical direction, the early sessions for these songs were still rough. The music would have to grow, and to help with that process, Bono had to reflect on his skills as a songwriter and grow as well. This meant getting out of his comfort zone and doing things differently than the band had done in the past. Recalling the need to change U2's music and songwriting process, Bono described that U2 never really wrote songs in any traditional sense and often considered writing lyrics to be outdated and insufficient for their process of making music. Typically for U2, as they had done on their albums prior to *The Joshua Tree*, they would just explore musical sounds and then build a composition from there, with Bono considering that U2 had just manipulated the sound of their music rather than working cohesively on writing songs. With Larry often being the driving force for U2 to focus more on the craft of songwriting during this time, the band would play together in jams and piece the songs together bit by bit. [Parkyn, *Touch the Flame*, 79]

In *U2 by U2*, Bono shares an anecdote that was meaningful to him and his development as a songwriter. On July 8, 1984, Bob Dylan wrapped up his 1984 European tour at Slane Castle, his first show in Ireland since 1966. Before the show, Bono interviewed Dylan for *Hot Press*. While meeting him, Bono was also introduced to Van Morrison, and the three discussed Irish music traditions and songwriting, with Bono feeling like a student in the presence of the pair of accomplished musical legends. Bono told Dylan and Morrison that U2 had no musical roots they drew from. He acknowledged that Ireland has a musical tradition, but it was not something U2 ever channeled, instead insisting that U2 existed within their own space. Dylan then urged Bono to reflect on his own heritage's musical history, insisting that Bono should look back to the traditional Irish groups of the past, a suggestion that would be a catalyst for Bono to reevaluate how U2 wrote and recorded songs. [McCormick and U2, *U2 by U2*, 155]

Dylan then asked Bono to perform with him on stage during the encore. Bono admitted that he was not familiar with much of Dylan's catalog before feigning that he knew "Blowin' in the Wind." During the performance of Dylan's iconic rhetorical song, he signaled for Bono to continue. Instead of singing the song's actual lyrics, Bono then improvised new lyrics singing

How many times must a bombsman last?
How many times must people cry?
How many newspapers must we read before we go to sleep?

As he continued, Bono repeated the question "How many times?" several times before closing the song with more improvisational lines such as

I want to see your heart shine
I want to see your faces
I want to see your hands wave
My friend, it's blowin' in the wind
It's blowin' in the wind.
[Greene, "Flashback"]

Between the interview with Dylan and not knowing one of the legendary songwriter's most famous songs, it reaffirmed that Bono had a lot to learn about the craftsmanship of songwriting. As part of his early songwriting process, Bono used to write lyrics separately from U2 believing that words had no place in rock music. He considered his method of songwriting as being akin to a sketch artist, quickly crafting something by throwing paint at a canvas and letting it drip. [Black, *Bono In His Own Words*, 39]

Despite the strange circumstance that allowed Bono to alter his song, Dylan remained close friends with him and introduced him to the great songwriting history of American and Irish folk music traditions, as well as contemporary artists who drew heavily from those traditions. According to Niall Stokes, Bono became fascinated with Bruce Springsteen, "opening another window into the blue-collar world of labour songs." [Stokes, *Into the Heart*, 71] In the spirit of exploring these traditions, U2 had also chosen to perform the Peggy Seeger song "Springhill Mining Disaster," a song about the exploitation of a Nova Scotian coal mine, for a 25th anniversary tribute to The Dubliners.

With a newfound approach to the songwriting process, coupled with the discovery of musical traditions of their own homeland and that of America's, U2 could continue to conceptualize their critique of America that would result in *The Joshua Tree*. "Red Hill Mining Town" would become the track from *The Joshua Tree* that, from a songwriting perspective, best represented the influence traditional American and Irish folk music had on U2. Despite the band's progress in crafting better songs, "Red Hill Mining Town" would also represent the band's growing pains as songwriters and musicians.

Inspired by Tony Parker's *Red Hill: A Mining Community*, a collection of oral histories from those involved with the National Union of Mineworkers strikes, "Red Hill Mining Town" was written about a struggling marriage. In an interview with Island Records, Bono told Carter Alan that the song was not just about the coal mining strikes but also the financial and emotional strain being unemployed has on a relationship and the potential fallout.

The lines of "Red Hill Mining Town" are brief, but they paint a portrait of a type of stoic, yet cracked, man dealing with the fallout of Thatcher's neoconservative economic policies intruding into his homelife. Though short in delivery, each line of the lyrics is meant to conjure up this image. Bono sings about blood running thin, split seams, coal-cracked faces, long lines, and the inability to turn back. These lines open the song and convey the image of picketers marching in the strike, with the wind blowing in their frozen faces. Not much is being said about the strike, but it gives a contextualized quality to the character of a coal miner as well as setting the scene for the heart of the drama within the song.

As the song progresses, Bono delivers lines that represent the miner returning home to his wife and family, burdened by the economic hardships of the strike. At this point of the song's narrative, Bono is creating a scene in which to understand how much the strike is fracturing the marriage and family dynamic. Bono recognized the enormous pressure the miners were under returning from the strike and having to raise their children and take care of their families, often straining their relationships to the point of breaking. [O'Hare, "The Secret History"] The scene that is carried out to illustrate this is of a miner, after drowning his sorrows in alcohol, returning to his cavern-like home where a cold void has taken the place of his wife's love. There is an acknowledged resignation that fear and doubt are responsible for the marriage's decline. Though, in that acknowledgment, there is a plea from the man. He can lose his job, which is one extent of his identity as a working-class father and husband, but the fear of losing the support and structure of his family is too much to bear, telling his wife he cannot live without her.

With the song's opening representing a picket line and then segueing into an intimate scene at home, the final verse combines the emotional character of both scenes into one that solidifies the song's narrative. Bono sings of the chains being undone as the links connecting this man's job, otherwise his livelihood, to his wife and his family become broken. In this narrative, it appears that the man waits for this scene all day from the picket lines, aware that it will come down on him like a hunter capturing prey when he returns home later in the evening. The chain link signifies the miner's emotional connection between his job and his family. The job, as a means to achieve economic stability, grants him the ability to support his family and fulfill his role as the provider, but losing one adversely affects his connection with the other. Bono would clarify the song's narrative in a 1987 interview with *NME* saying that although the miners' strike interested him from a political perspective, he was more concerned with the subject on a deeper and personal level. Bono did not feel that parroting the story of the mining pits closing, though tragic, conveyed the heart of the human story present in the struggle the miners and their families faced. With "Red Hill Mining Town," he wanted to explore what happened at home and channeled the strain the family was under. Many miners could not face their wives and children because of their pride and that was the essence of what Bono wanted to capture. [Thrills, "Cactus World View"]

The most interesting aspect of the song's lyrics are the lines, performed in spoken word by Bono, exposing the conflict of morality within coal mining and its impact, implying effects on both natural environments and society. With these lines, Bono suggests that man has scorched the Earth and set the sky ablaze in our desire to gain more but at the expense of something far greater. These lines illustrate the compromises that are made for the sake of progress. The listener imagines smoke-filled skies and land devastated by industrialization, symbolizing the price we pay for progress, and those being representative of humanity's choice to destroy our own well-being for convenience. However, given that Bono's focus on "Red Hill Mining Town" is about what happens to the miners when they return home from the picket lines, these lines could also represent a miner's conscience as they reconcile the impact their occupation and the strike has on their personal life. It is clever imagery that merges the issues of environmental and emotional devastation coal miners faced during this time.

Though the origin of "Red Hill Mining Town" culminated from the band's exploration of traditional American and Irish folk music, which have storied traditions that often rely on gender tropes to drive the narrative, the wives of miners involved in the real-life strikes were not as emotionally cold and fragile as they appear to be in the song. The women in these miners' lives were extremely important sources of support during the strike. Chapters of the Women's Action Group organized to support the striking miners by providing aid through soup kitchens, distributing resources, and even actively participating in picket lines where violent confrontations from police were a possibility. These women also held their own rallies, such as the National Women Against Pit Closures rally, to condemn Thatcher's economic policies and to collect donations of food and goods, such as Christmas presents, for the miners and their families.

The image of a strained marriage in the song was likely a reflection of Bono's own marriage under pressure. Regarding his wife, Bono asserts that Ali is an independent person and will not be worn like a brooch. [Cocks, "U2: Band on the Run"] U2's touring schedule during the mid-1980s and the early recording sessions of *The Joshua Tree* put enormous strain on Bono, which adversely affected his marriage. Bono felt his life was in disarray as he struggled to find balance between his life as a husband and life as a rock star.

Considering that U2 were driven to enhance their own musicality to take them into a new direction, Bono likely drew from his own personal experience to write "Red Hill Mining Town." Though he expressed that he was politically interested in the strike, it was the relationship aspect he wanted to explore in the song because he felt unqualified to comment on the strike in any deeply political fashion, focusing rather on the drama of the relationship because he understood that dynamic more than the life of a miner working in a pit. [Graham and Stokes, "U2 Give Themselves Away"] Through the difficulty Bono was experiencing in his marriage at the time, it can be reasoned that he embodied the miner in the song with Ali being the only thing left to hold on to before, as in the song's conclusion, love slowly strips away as the lights go down on Red Hill Town.

Though the narrative of "Red Hill Mining Town" was set against the backdrop of the National Union of Mineworkers strikes, many criticized U2 for the song's lack of an obvious political statement. Bono was more interested in the fallout that followed from thousands losing their jobs than he was about becoming a voice for a political movement. [Stokes, "The World About Us"]

Though U2 has undeniably garnered a reputation as being a political band, until "Bullet the Blue Sky" on *The Joshua Tree*, the band was often not specific regarding their political stances within their songs. Although classic songs like "Sunday Bloody Sunday," with Bono waving a white flag and declaring the anthem was not a rebel song during U2's 1983 live concert album and video *Under a Blood Red Sky*, reinforce a belief of U2's political nature, that is a narrative that is applied with hindsight. There was often ambiguity that left enough room for critics and audiences to criticize, or even be confused by, U2 for their lack of an overt political statement in their music.

Making *The Joshua Tree* presented U2 with the opportunity to start thinking more broadly about music being a tool to communicate a clear and concise political message. Their existential journey through American politics and culture helped them expand on this ability, by strengthening their songwriting and delving into musical traditions, to convey ideas that were more holistic in tone and delivery. When the band took a break from recording to perform as part of Amnesty International's A Conspiracy of Hope tour, it was a revelatory experience for U2 and validated this newfound inspiration to develop their new musical and political direction for *The Joshua Tree*. It became imperative for them to shine a light on Reagan's greed by injecting an edginess into the music and lyrics of the album that illustrated what they were seeing. [McCormick and U2, *U2 by U2*, 174]

During the recording of *The Joshua Tree*, U2 would become more comfortable and brazen with the political commentary within their music to express their ideals and critique anything or anyone that undermined those ideals. Prior to this album, when Bono had believed words had no place in rock music, perhaps he felt U2 had lacked the skill, or even willingness, to make a definitive stand. Now, in this era of unabashed neoconservatism, it became essential to learn how to craft songs to address the problems U2 had with Reagan and Thatcher. Although "Red Hill Mining Town" was not overt in its political commentary, being one of the earliest songs U2 began working on for *The Joshua Tree*, it helped pave the way for U2 to have the confidence to write and record songs with an apparent, and eventually obvious, political message.

Though "Red Hill Mining Town" represented U2's new interest in finding inspiration through folk music traditions to improve their songwriting, the history of the song's recording is peculiar and unlike that of any other song on *The Joshua Tree*. In *U2 by U2*, Larry described "Red Hill Mining Town" as being a song that had a lot of great elements but was difficult to finalize and that too much time was spent on the production and not enough on writing the song. Larry said Bono had a vision for the song and how it would sound, but no one else seemed to understand. U2's knack for improvisation resulted in a lot of interesting qualities, but Larry said no one felt sure about the direction of the song. They were too close to the material and insecure about pushing as far in this new direction as they could have. Though "Red Hill Mining Town" contained a lot of great qualities that excited the band, it was ultimately viewed as underdeveloped despite it appearing on *The Joshua Tree*. Larry believed their improvisational approach generated a lot of interesting ideas but presented obstacles as well. [McCormick and U2, *U2 by U2*, 184]

In hindsight, although Larry describes "Red Hill Mining Town" as one of *The Joshua Tree*'s lost songs, that certainly was not the case in 1987 when U2 initially wanted the song to be the album's second single following "With or Without You." In support of this decision, they even went as far as to film a music video for the song helmed by Neil Jordan, director of *The Crying Game*, which featured the band performing in a coal mine, sweaty and surrounded by canaries. Lou Maglia, president of Island Records at the time, was adamant that "I Still Haven't Found What I'm Looking For" be released as the album's second single, going as far as mailing copies of the single to radio disc jockeys where it was met with positive reviews and heavy airplay. Despite their insisting that "Red Hill Mining Town" be released, U2 reluctantly shelved the single.

Perhaps one reason why "Red Hill Mining Town" would be considered a lost gem for the band was the fact that, until The Joshua Tree Tour 2017, it was the only song from *The Joshua Tree* that was never performed live. During an interview on BBC Radio 2, Bono told Chris Evans why the band never played the song live. Bono said that he had a habit of writing songs that he could not adequately sing in a live setting but was unbothered by it because sometimes his straining to hit the notes was part of the emotional drama of the song and its narrative. However, Bono would feel physically unable to perform the song again at the next show, so he felt it was better to leave a song like "Red Hill Mining Town" off the setlist until he could learn how to sing it better. [Evans, interview]

Bono's vocal struggle to perform the song in a live setting does speak to the lack of confidence Larry suggested the band had about it when originally recording it, but so does the fact that U2 released "Red Hill Mining Town" as a single in 2017 with a new mix. Steve Lillywhite, who produced the 2017 mix, told *Variety* that U2 never finished the song the way they had intended, thinking that it always could have been improved upon from what appeared on *The Joshua Tree*. [Halperin, "Bono"] For the song's new mix, the changes Lillywhite made were to re-record Bono's vocals and, most notably, bring out the song's brass accompaniment, which was buried in the original album for being out of tune and with synthesizers emphasized in its place. Finally pleased with the new mix of *The Joshua Tree*'s lost single, it was released as a picture vinyl disc for Record Store Day in 2017, 30 years after U2 initially fought for its release.

"Red Hill Mining Town" was first performed live on the opening night of The Joshua Tree Tour 2017. Despite being a tour that contextualized the relevance of *The Joshua Tree*'s political and social commentary amid America's existential crisis under Donald Trump, U2 chose to depoliticize the song in its live setting. Instead, the video projection screen augmented the song with a performance by a Salvation Army brass band, signifying U2's confidence that they eventually got "Red Hill Mining Town" right, on a musical level, three decades later by nodding to the brass section buried in the song's original album mix. Although it was great for U2 to feel confident in their abilities 30 years after recording *The Joshua Tree*, an album that represents a journey and everything within it both good and bad, it was a missed opportunity to make the themes of "Red Hill Mining Town" relevant in a current context. Though, considering that the album did also reflect a journey of musical and personal discovery, perhaps one cannot be too harsh toward U2 for taking 30 years to complete that part of their journey. Some things are worth holding on to.

Chapter Twelve

Bed of Nails

When U2 finished The Unforgettable Fire tour during summer 1985, they began working on the early sessions for what would become *The Joshua Tree* that fall. They were now full-fledged rock stars with all the fame, glory, and temptation that came with that. Now world-renowned, it was key for the band to capitalize on this new success and status by getting back to work by creating a follow-up to *The Unforgettable Fire* that would exceed audiences' expectations as well as their own. The pressure, from the band's work commitments and the allure of rock stardom sin that comes with fame, was getting to Bono and forcing him into a vulnerable place. During this time, although Bono would be coy about U2's increasing fame by describing himself as only a part-time rock star, this new lifestyle would have a full-time effect on his personal life.

Since their earliest days as a band, U2 were always struggling with fame and their identities as rock stars. Around the time of recording their second studio album *October* in 1981, the band had a crisis of faith as they were pressured by a Christian group named the Shalom Fellowship, of which everyone but Adam was a member of, to abandon their rock star ambitions and commit themselves to their faith. Trying to reconcile whether they could still be Christians if they pursued a career in music, they felt enough strain to the point of almost quitting their musical aspirations. Once they resolved for themselves the issue of whether practicing Christians could be rock stars, other existential conflicts arose. As their success and profile as a band grew, they struggled at times reconciling their reasons for being in a band and, according to Bono, "to not let being in the band destroy our lives and marriages." [Doyle, "American Dreams" 80] Now, several years later and U2 on their way to being the biggest rock group on the planet, Bono had to resolve a crisis once again for himself, one that forced him to reconcile his art with his marriage.

While recording *The Joshua Tree*, Bono was experiencing deeply difficult emotional issues, not fully realizing his own freedom while being married. [Doyle, "American Dreams" 80] In *U2: The Definitive Biography*, Jobling cites that Bono's marriage was strained because of U2's commitments as a band, from recording to touring, as well as the physical distance between him and Ali, who was attending Dublin University College to study social and political sciences. [Jobling, *U2*, 162–63] With all the touring and increased attention that came with their fame, there were now more opportunities for the kind of temptation that typical rock stars were privy to. In *U2 by U2*, Bono expressed a vulnerability exposing the "pure torment" he was feeling at the time. It was during the recording of *The Joshua Tree*, when U2 reached new heights of their fame, that Bono was attempting to reconcile an internal conflict between staying committed to his career and music and staying committed to his wife. Aware of his own personal qualities and flaws, such as his nomadic thoughts, Bono felt compelled to reconcile two different paths to wander down: one of domesticity and one of rock star liberation. [McCormick and U2, *U2 by U2*, 181]

Temptation is a consistent theme throughout *The Joshua Tree* and appears in a variety of different contexts. Temptation to violently react against power and political oppression is expressed in U2's condemnation of US foreign policy in "Bullet the Blue Sky." The macabre narrative of "Exit" deals with the temptation to seek violent retribution for being forced to live on the fringes of the American Dream. The bluesy romp "Trip Through Your Wires," with its narrative of sexual temptation, is the story of being saved by a woman whose salvation could be illusory. For "With or Without You," U2's first number-one single, temptation is something to overcome through a personal, and even religious, journey to seek balance.

Writing lyrics for *The Joshua Tree* was a considerable challenge for Bono. Bono had to reevaluate his process as a songwriter and the role lyrics played in elevating a song's meaning. During the sessions for *The Joshua Tree*, his songwriting became a therapeutic release to deal with the struggles in his personal life. With writing "With or Without You," it became an exercise to abandon ego and really think about the emotional and spiritual complexities of a committed relationship. Although much of *The Joshua Tree* was initially conceptualized to be an existential journey through America, noting its hypocrisies and beauty, Bono embarking on a personal journey became an aspect of U2's overall pilgrimage through America. There was a darkness U2 discovered in America that became a reflection of Bono's own darkness and his anxieties with temptation as a rock star.

Bono described this internal struggle, saying, "so now I have this person in my life whom I love more than my life but I'm wondering if the reason I'm not writing is because I'm now a domesticated beast." Not limiting himself to just black-and-white thoughts concerning being unfaithful in his marriage, the whole idea of having a family while being a major rock star was something Bono had to grapple with, an issue to resolve by striking a balance if indeed one was possible for him. It was during this time he often felt himself exposed and vulnerable to the consequences of his own wandering spirit, including having been taken advantage of by people close to him. Writing "With or Without You" was a realization that Bono still had much to learn about himself and his identity. [McCormick and U2, *U2 by U2*, 181]

The song's evolution stemmed from the rest of U2 becoming frustrated with the quality of Bono's lyrics. "[Bono] had a whole set of lyrics for most of the album but [U2] weren't happy with them," said Dave Meegan, assistant engineer for *The Joshua Tree*. "They were really critical of Bono at the time and they sent him off to rewrite them all, and what he came back with was just absolutely stunning." [Jobling, *U2*, 164]

"With or Without You" was one of the first songs U2 worked on during the early sessions for *The Joshua Tree* at Larry's house during late 1985. The songs during the initial stages of the album's development were essentially just jams and demos. The Edge described "With or Without You" starting off as a terrible chord pattern during this early point. [McCormick and U2, *U2 by U2*, 172] Larry was often the toughest with the band according to Meegan, describing that Larry would often let the rest of the band know if what they were doing sounded awful. Meegan suggested that Larry's disinterest in an idea would result in the idea being completely abandoned. [Jobling, *U2*, 164–65]

Due to the pushback he was receiving from the rest of the band, Bono continued to work on "With or Without You" with the help of his friend Gavin Friday, founding member of The Virgin Prunes. The song's signature chord sequence came from Bono, but Friday worked on organizing and structuring the song and, with the aid of Brian Eno's sequencer, gave it an arpeggiated flair. Adam reflected on the experience, recalling Bono's chord sequence as being fairly conventional and repetitive. The band felt stuck with this element of the song and not knowing in which direction to take it before ultimately continuing to work on it by adding a drum machine and bass. [McCormick and U2, *U2 by U2*, 179–81]

While Bono and Friday were working on the song's overall structure, the Edge was working with a guitar prototype provided to him called the Infinite Guitar. Designed and built by Michael Brook, the Infinite Guitar was created to sustain a note infinitely. How the Infinite Guitar achieves this is by taking an electronic circuit from a standard pickup and then amplifying the signal as it is fed into a separate feedback coil. The Edge joked about the Infinite Guitar's specific instructions and how "this piece of gear would have failed even the most basic of safety regulations" and often led the Edge, or his guitar technician, to get electrocuted. [McCormick and U2, *U2 by U2*, 179–81]

The inclusion of the Infinite Guitar during the recording of "With or Without You" resulted in a breakthrough moment that excited, yet puzzled, the band. The Edge was tooling with the instrument's sustain while Friday and Bono were working in the control room playing the drum and bass tracks. As the sounds from the two rooms intermingled, the Edge recalled the others claiming "That's it! But what the fuck is it?" According to Bono, he called for the Edge and immediately started to record him performing on the Infinite Guitar. [McCormick and U2, *U2 by U2*, 181]

The impasse U2 was experiencing, according to the Edge, was causing the band to struggle in searching for the right arrangement. Until this coincidence in the studio, the individual parts that would eventually combine to make "With or Without You" were just elements that frustrated the band because they had no idea where they each fit in. Although many of the other songs from *The Joshua Tree* originated from improvisation and jam sessions, of which the original demo for "With or Without You" was poorly received, recording the song involved a methodical process that was unusual for the band. Lanois said that "With or Without You" did not stem from a performance from the band but rather became something manufactured in the studio's control room. [Mirkin, "With or Without You"] Now that the music for "With or Without You" was coming together, even though accidentally, Bono was able to find the right way to express the pain he was feeling over his relationship. He describes the song as being "about torment, sexual but also psychological, about how repressing desires makes them stronger." [McCormick and U2, *U2 by U2*, 181] With the band critiquing Bono's songs and forcing him to write better lyrics, Bono was driven to distill his emotions into their purest form and create something that would be meaningful to him but also serve as an emotional release. The song evokes feelings of masochism, yearning, and the complicated and complex mixture of the two through Bono conveying torturous desire through imagery of a bed of nails, a bruised body, and a twisting thorn. They all come together to create the "pure torment" Bono described as he rationalized his desires as an artist against his obligations as a husband. The struggle is illustrated through the push and pull of one's own needs and the needs of a partner. Stuck trying to find a balance, there is a surrender of the ego as Bono sings that he cannot live with or without the love of his life.

Although the lyrics of "With or Without You" convey the intermingling of love and desire, the lines with the most significance, as they relate to Bono's personal journey, are his repeating of giving himself away. In *Walk On: The Spiritual Journey of U2*, Steve Stockman discusses the religious symbolism of the line connecting it with Luke 9:24, which, in the King James Version of the Christian Bible, says, "For whosoever will save his life shall lose it: but whosoever will lose his life for my sake, the same shall save it." Stockman suggests that, although love and marriage are reasons why one may give themselves away, it also represents the notion that this surrender "could be spiritual or even opening up to hundreds of thousands of fans every night." [Stockman, *Walk On*, 81]

Stockman's assessment regarding the meaning of Bono giving himself away adds analytical depth to Bono's personal struggle while recording the song. Bono did suggest that this experience was not strictly about sexual infidelity but rather finding the balance between all of his responsibilities and obligations within his band and his marriage.

I see the significance of giving one's self away as being a statement about sacrifice and the difficult decisions that come with that. Although Bono had a desire for U2 to be a successful rock band, he also had other people in his life outside of the band who had been with him since U2's beginning, namely his wife Ali. U2 were at a crossroads after their 1985 performance at Live Aid and generally had not previously considered themselves as rock stars, so Bono's temptation and flirting with the life-style's excesses were a product of that newfound success. Their journey through the dichotomy of America also, for Bono, meant reconciling his anxiety of that success with his journey through the American mythos. He had to give something away or else have it taken away from him.

About this line, Bono said in *Hot Press* that he often felt exposed and that the band felt he would give himself away to the point that any damage done to U2 would be because Bono would become too vulnerable and open himself up too much. This self-awareness got to a point where Bono felt motivated to consider not doing any interviews because the damage to his personal life could be too great. [Stokes, "The World About Us"]

In their essay "The Authentic Self in Paul Riceour and U2," Jeffrey F. Keuss and Sara Koenig analyze Bono's struggle in "With or Without You" through Riceour's philosophy as well as analyze U2's music and its inherent metaphors of "illustrating authentic personhood." Citing Riceour's concept of "self-apophasis," a recognition by an individual of their own emptiness in relation to another with whom they release themselves for love, is the result of when an identity is forged in addition to self-constancy. [Keuss and Koenig, "The Authentic Self," 59–61]

Keuss and Koenig acknowledge that Riceour's concept of self-apophasis is seen throughout Christianity by analyzing the religion's concept of Purgatio, known as purgation. Purgatio, one of the three levels of the Christian faith preceding illuminatio (illumination) and unitio (union), signifies the role of prayer, practice, and tradition, all three being strengths provided by the Holy Spirit in resisting and seeking control of sinful desires. Within "With or Without You," Keuss and Koenig acknowledge Bono's struggle to "seek union with the lover," an act that may require his death as illustrated through Bono's internal conflict of being unable to live with or without his lover. [Keuss and Koenig, "The Authentic Self," 59–61] Within the scope of Riceour's self-apophasis as applied to "With or Without You" illustrated by Keuss and Koenig, Bono must resolve this conflict by deciding whether to purge the source of this conflict to embrace the lover, a manifestation of the true self. With this inherent struggle of being unable to live with or without his lover, there is an active resolution to decide how to become that true self. By giving himself away, of purging what torments him, Bono is embracing the idea of being more complete. It is this juncture where Bono decides what will make him feel more complete as a true representation of his identity and what path to take after purgation that affects his relationship with the lover and how he sees himself in relation.

With this "violence of love," as Bono describes it, he is seeing for himself and the people around him that "love is a two-edged sword." Bono elaborates on this, saying, "I didn't want to write about romance because that doesn't interest me as much as the other side." [Jobling, *U2*, 163] This other side Bono speaks of is the complexities of love, his own personal struggle, and the necessary act of surrendering ego. What Stockman, Keuss, and Koenig are saying, through their inclusion of religion in the song's narrative, is that there is also a spiritual element to the act of giving one's self away that is an outward or external expression that is not necessarily separate from one that is more inward and internal. The idea of Bono giving himself away to find a healthy balance between his music and marriage may be driven by his own personal desires. It is within the foundation of these theological tenets that drive Bono's sense of self and identifies the source of the struggles that could potentially lead him astray from achieving that sense of self. What he gives away impacts what he is bound to lose or gain, an act that allows Bono to live up to and embody a measure of his true self as a resolution to his internal conflict within "With or Without You."

"With or Without You" was released as the first single from *The Joshua Tree* despite the band feeling doubtful about its commercial and radio appeal. Adam said releasing the song was an act of challenging commercial radio because the song, on a sonic and compositional level, did not sound like other singles topping the charts in March 1987. Although U2 were reluctant to release the song as a single, and their manager Paul McGuinness was adamant about not releasing it as a single, it was Gavin Friday who championed the song's release. Friday got into one of the biggest arguments he had ever had with McGuiness, when he suggested that "With or Without You" would be a guaranteed number-one single, with Bono ultimately siding with him. [*Hot Press*, "Reach Out and Touch the Flame"]

In Jobling's *U2: The Definitive Biography*, Dave Meegan shared his initial experience with "With or Without You," recalling Bono bringing in the song's mix from Windmill Lane Studios and encouraging him to listen to it because he was unsure if it was any good. Meegan was thrilled by the mix and told Bono the song would hit number one on the charts all over the world. Meegan felt that the members of U2 were too close to the tracks they were recording for *The Joshua Tree* thus they were unable to see the value and quality of the music they were creating. [Jobling, *U2*, 165]

Since being released as a single and earning their first number one, U2 have included "With or Without You" as a concert staple on most tours since its premiere during the second show of The Joshua Tree tour on April 4, 1987. Over the years, the song has been performed with various modifiers including snippets of other songs or extra lyrics with Bono singing about him and his lover under stars shining in summer nights or winter light, united through one heart, hope, and love.

During The Joshua Tree Tour 2017, U2 performed the song as various panoramas of desert landscapes appeared on the projection screen. During the song's outro, Bono would dedicate it to lovers of song and to lovers in songs, urging them to sing their hearts out. The performance on this tour was meant to celebrate love against the backdrop of a scenic splendor that inspired the concept of *The Joshua Tree*, the desert of America's heartland and the hidden beauty within it.

Though other songs from the album would use that same desert landscape concept to critique America's flawed dichotomy, and extend that to Trump within a modern context for the 2017 tour, the significance of "With or Without You" on The Joshua Tree Tour 2017 was to remember the love and beauty that America can offer and that it has the potential to offer more of that to more people, at least when it abandons the ego of its own divisiveness to actualize the true self it could be. It suggested that the symbolism of this beauty, and what it represented existentially, is worth fighting for against the tyranny of oppressors, specifically Trump, whose administration championed authoritarian values that undermined many Americans. "With or Without You" is not a political song but, in the context of the 30th anniversary tour, it gave life to the idea that love can be a political act.

Chapter Thirteen

Bleed for It

ONE OF THE MORE DIFFICULT ASPECTS OF ANY JOURNEY, WHETHER they be larger explorations of a country's mythos or individual ones of self-discovery, is that there will be times when the path is unclear. It is then we often find ourselves misguided, confused, and full of doubt as these obstacles keep us from a truth we are seeking. People come in and out of our lives, temporarily joined as they share their journey with us, as we move forward and learn from our experiences and use the knowledge gained from them. Sometimes, these people stay with us for many miles. Others, they are gone too soon, though our memory keeps them with us every step of the way.

It was during The Unforgettable Fire tour in 1984 that U2 visited Australia and New Zealand for the first time, which initiated, according to Bono, a feeling of deep admiration for the two Oceanian nations. Unable to sleep due to jet lag after the 24-hour flight to Auckland, Bono rose out of his hotel bed at 2 a.m. and visited the lobby where he noticed some people sitting at the bar who caught his attention, and he introduced himself to them. After telling them that he did not know anyone in Auckland, they took him out to One Tree Hill.

Maungakiekie, the indigenous name for One Tree Hill, is a volcanic peak in Auckland that serves as a memorial place for the Māori people. When Bono visited, a single tree stood at the top (it has since been destroyed as a result of Māori activists taking chainsaws to it to protest injustices perpetuated by the New Zealand government against the indigenous population). Bono was struck by the scene saying it resembled the starkness of a Japanese painting. Looking over the volcanic craters and the Auckland skyline, Bono said that the area evoked feelings of freedom for him. The scene was making Bono self-aware about his own identity and the limitations he had forced on himself, recognizing that he was far away from home and any number of things could happen to him. This visit to Maungakiekie instilled in Bono the realization that he had always been "disappearing into other people's lives," [McCormick and U2, *U2 by U2*, 157] an epiphany that continued to shape his own personal journey of self-discovery and search for balance. U2 were still well over a year away from beginning to conceptualize *The Joshua Tree* at this point, but Bono's thoughts that night in Auckland were an early indication of the journey he would embark on for the album.

One of the people in that group was Greg Carroll, a local Māori man who had started his career in the New Zealand music scene at age 20 working with bands such as Straight Flash. While U2 were touring in New Zealand to support *The Unforgettable Fire*, Carroll was hired as a stagehand. Described as "lithe, quick on his feet, sharp and with a real light of intelligence in his eyes" by Bono, Carroll was soon hired to join U2's touring crew for the "Under Australian Skies" leg of The Unforgettable Fire tour in Australia. Carroll had never been out of his native home of New Zealand before, so U2 acquired him a passport to work with the band in Australia before touring in America. [McCormick and U2, *U2 by U2*, 177] When the tour concluded, Carroll was hired as U2's assistant and brought with him for the flight to Dublin, according to the band's guitar technician Stephen Rainford, "only a plastic bag for his clothes." [Jobling, *U2*, 156]

While working in Dublin as U2's assistant, Carroll developed a close friendship with Bono to the point of being considered a brother and became a respected member of the U2 camp. In *U2 by U2*, Bono recalled the close relationship he developed with Carroll, as well as the impact his presence and influence had on the rest of U2. Carroll's warmth also extended to their families, with Bono remembering that he became very close to his wife Ali, often taking her and the band members' other wives out dancing and treating them exceptionally well. [McCormick and U2, *U2 by U2*, 157]

With every journey, though, there is the certainty that one's faith and resilience will be tested—a darkness that threatens to alter the path or even throw one off course. It is during these difficult times that we discover new facets of our identity, sometimes connecting with our past, that alter how we continue onward. During his own existential journey, it was a chance encounter that enlightened Bono with a renewed sense of self and granted him a friend to share that experience with, but it was also chance that brought that part of his journey to a screeching halt.

On July 3, 1986, at age 26, Carroll was killed in a motorcycle accident in Dublin's city center, hitting a car directly head-on as it pulled out in front of him. Carroll's death significantly affected the members of U2. It was the first time anyone associated with the band had been killed. [McCormick and U2, *U2 by U2*, 177] The Edge said Carroll's death should have been avoidable but was just a freakish occurrence. Adam described the incident as quite a sobering experience for U2 and their team. However, the person most impacted by Carroll's death was Bono, the one closest to him. Bono described that Carroll's death was traumatic for him and he felt guilty because Carroll was riding his motorcycle after running an errand for him.

Carroll's body was flown from Ireland to New Zealand where it could experience his tangihanga, or tangi, a traditional Māori funeral rite held on a marae, a scared ground. Carroll's tangi was held for three days and three nights at Kai-iwi Marae near his homeland of Whanganui. According to John Jobling, Bono read a poem to more than 200 people in attendance at Carroll's tangi and said that Carroll "believed in New Zealand, believed in his Māori background" and that the U2 camp "all believed in him." [Jobling, *U2*, 156–57] During the tangi, Bono performed The Beatles' "Let It Be" and Bob Dylan's "Knockin' On Heaven's Door." Bono, reflecting on Carroll's tangi, said it was beyond belief watching Carroll being buried by his tribal homeland elders and that it made it feel as if his head kept spinning. [Graham and Stokes, "U2 Give Themselves Away"] It was Carroll's tangi that inspired Bono to write "One Tree Hill," a tribute to his beloved friend and the special place they shared together.

"One Tree Hill," though a tribute to Carroll, represented U2 reconciling with the grim aspects of their personal journey while recording *The Joshua Tree*, a necessary step in understanding mortality and the need to break through darkness. For Adam, Carroll's death made him become aware about the things in life more important than his career in rock music, a dark lesson reminding him that time with friends and family is limited. [Graham and Stokes, "U2 Give Themselves Away"]

Carroll's death hit Bono the hardest. Not only did he lose a cherished friend, but Carroll's death forced him to revisit a traumatic experience from his past, one that shaped his identity as a budding artist which had now returned, influencing the recording of *The Joshua Tree* as well as U2's existential journey in the process. In *U2 by U2*, Bono associated Carroll's death with the tragic loss of his mother during his youth, saying,

> I guess the problem with dealing with death, for me, is that it's always the same death. It's always my mother dying. It's always the center of the universe disappearing and having to find another one. It just brings me back to that moment every time. It was a very big

event in the life of a small community here. The big subjects seem to be things that we always have to be reminded of. That's what our band seems to be about, and that just sort of set it off, it brought gravitas to the recording of *The Joshua Tree*. We had to fill the hole in our heart with something very, very large indeed, we loved him very much. [McCormick and U2, *U2 by U2*, 178]

The lyrics of "One Tree Hill" are multifaceted, covering various ideas and experiences Bono connected with Carroll. Of the most literal, closing the first verse, is Bono recounting first meeting Carroll and him singing about looking at the moon over One Tree Hill and the sun, in Carroll's eyes, going down. It is a poetic reflection of two memorable moments Bono experienced with Carroll, their meeting and his passing away.

Bono juxtaposes that serenity of meeting Carroll with a scene that highlights the intensity of his grief that alters his perception of Maungakiekie. At the place that brought him a sense of freedom, there is now a cold chill with mourners standing in a sun so bright that no one leaves any shadows. Where once he saw freedom in the volcanic terrain, he now only sees scars. Bono sings of the day begging for night to bring mercy, with the moon overhead as the sun in Carroll's eyes sets—a cry out and desire for relief from his bereavement.

In the second verse, Bono strays from the scene with Carroll to sing about Victor Jara, the activist who protested Augusto Pinochet's regime and was later killed after the 1973 Chilean coup d'état. Along with "Mothers of the Disappeared" and "Bullet the Blue Sky," Adam considered "One Tree Hill" part of a trilogy of songs that ruminate on death. While the other two songs deal with death as a political statement, there is nothing about Carroll's death that is rooted in these politics. Though, there is a deeper message of love and humanism in the lyrics of "One Tree Hill" that perhaps reflects the joy Carroll brought to U2.

Bono sings of a heart of darkness where poets are put to death for speaking their truth. Jara, who used folk music as a political weapon, preached a message of love, peace, and social justice that still resonates today, which Bono describes in terms of his blood crying from the ground. Despite so much death inherent within the narrative of *The Joshua Tree*, these lines, while seemingly out of place at first listen, represent U2's hope and optimism about the lingering and liberating power of ideals, an acknowledgment of the freedom Bono felt at Maungakiekie with Carroll.

In the song's final verse, Bono combines thematic elements of the first two verses regarding his grief for Carroll and juxtaposes it with the death and politics of Jara. In the first lines of this verse, Bono declares that he believes in neither painted roses nor bleeding hearts when bullets are causing so much devastation that they are raping the night. The painted roses could refer to the artifice of meaningless and empty gestures or even the murals painted by Jara's fellow Chileans of the Brigada Orlando Letelier which sometimes included roses, while the bleeding hearts represent Bono's cynicism toward seemingly well-intentioned people who speak about injustices that have yet to be resolved, all the while as he wrestles with his anger and grief. Combining the imagery of the roses, hearts, and bullets, the idea is that Bono is trying to assuage his own exhaustion of death and dismisses the rationalization of the naive or misleading sentiments of others who do not know or understand his feelings and experiences with death.

These lines refer to Bono's respect and admiration for Jara and his protests against Pinochet as they relate to U2's examination of America in *The Joshua Tree*. Bono is criticizing the civil rights and humanitarian crises in Central and South America, abetted by the US government. He dismisses the hypocritical notion of the US government espousing Christian ideals to paint their military and political interventions in a positive light that distract from the human rights abuses carried out in those regions.

Bono closes the verse singing that he will see Carroll again when the stars are falling and the moon over One Tree Hill has turned red, a desire to escape the specter of death that followed him throughout the recording of *The Joshua Tree* from his experiences in Central America and Ethiopia through the grieving of a close friend. Since his mother's untimely passing, death is a concept Bono returns to over and over again and it permeates throughout *The Joshua Tree*. Writing "One Tree Hill," Bono acknowledged that death has followed him throughout his life, delivering him a deep chill, and that he wishes to never experience it again. [Irwin, "This Is What We Do Best"]

Though, it is within the chorus that the song's most striking lines appear with Bono singing about running like a river to the sea. Niall Stokes suggests these lines connect Carroll's death "with themes of renewal and redemption." [Stokes, *Into the Heart*, 75] Although Bono has experienced a lot of anguish throughout his life, the anguish throughout "One Tree Hill," and *The Joshua Tree* as a whole, is overshadowed by hope. This hope comes from a recognition of overcoming personal tragedies and letting go through emotional farewells. Toward the end, there is an emotional release as Bono wails and vocalizes his intense grief expressed with the imagery of rain in his heart. After a brief pause, a coda fades in featuring a trio of "electro-acoustic" Raad strings, developed by musicians Dick, Paul, and Adele Armin, as backing vocals join Bono performing a farewell to Carroll as he runs to the sea, U2's grief washing away with the tide. [*Toronto Star*, "Trio Gives U2"]

As with many other songs on *The Joshua Tree*, the music for "One Tree Hill" originated during a jam session. The Edge described the jam's groove as being similar to highlife, a genre of music originating in present-day Ghana. Though not African in its delivery but rather considerably elaborate, the Edge recalled that U2 had never anticipated in their wildest dreams that they could sound like they did when recording the track.

Musically, the most stunning and remarkable aspect of "One Tree Hill" is Bono's vocals as he delivers this tribute to his dear friend—perhaps the best vocal performance on the entire album. Recorded in one take, Bono was too emotionally raw to perform a second, reflecting on the experience during a 1987 interview saying that U2 had never performed "One Tree Hill" before and that he just could not muster the emotional strength to do it again. He recalled that it is a song he has listened to many times but has not truly heard because of the pain he associates with it, so much so to the point that he had cut himself off from the song and removed himself from it. [Breskin, interview]

Beyond the scope of "One Tree Hill," Carroll's death played a larger role in developing the overall theme and aesthetic of *The Joshua Tree*, connecting it with the complex imagery of the desert. Although the desert provides the cinematic backdrop throughout *The Joshua Tree*, with it even being the narrative focal point for some songs, "One Tree Hill" derives inspiration from the concept in less obvious ways, serving to illustrate the extreme conditions one may encounter during a journey of self-discovery.

For Bono, 1986 was a difficult year as a result of Carroll's death. Losing him became a terrible time for the band and was the reason why Bono was so drawn to the desert as an image. [Irwin, "This Is What We Do Best"] Such as with his epiphany when writing "Where the Streets Have No Name," Bono sought out and wandered through the desert where, emotionally and spiritually parched, he would meet God and realize who he was.

Reminded of his mother's death, and forced to relive that trauma through Carroll's, Bono had to introspectively think about the role death played in his art. Though he described friends and family emphasizing to him that he had to focus on how much he had, such as a number-one album as part of a hugely successful rock band, as opposed to how much he lost, he fully comprehended just how much he had lost with Carroll and how much he continued to feel that loss. [Stokes, "The World About Us"]

The significance of the desert, as it relates to Carroll's death, is the difficulty of surviving the journey through the harshness of a barren land and the potential enlightenment that comes from overcoming its brutality. It is a landscape where one has to shed excess, void of anything that is not humanly essential, and open oneself to the wisdom that can be gained from the experience. *The Joshua Tree* as a whole is an album about the band's existential journey through a dichotomous America, but within that larger theme are multiple trials and tribulations that serve as obstacles and hardships that distract from the main purpose, pushing in another direction. Feelings of doubt and pain from Carroll's death permeated throughout the remainder of *The Joshua Tree* recording sessions, and it took perseverance for U2 to continue with the vision for their album. Their journey through the deserts of the American heartland and their own personal journeys would leave scars, reminders of the challenges they conquered.

Released on March 9, 1987, *The Joshua Tree* was dedicated to Carroll, with "One Tree Hill" exclusively released as a single in Australia and New Zealand a year later. During The Joshua Tree tour, the song would not be performed live until the third leg of the tour, in North America, because Bono was still healing from the tragedy. The song was performed in shows throughout Australia and New Zealand for the Lovetown tour in 1989 but had been rarely performed since until its inclusion during the entirety of The Joshua Tree Tour 2017.

The performances of "One Tree Hill" during The Joshua Tree Tour 2017 were prefaced by Bono with messages of remembrance, not just for Carroll but for all the people in the audience who lost loved ones too early. During a performance in Rome, Bono said that being in the Eternal City made him aware of the passing of time and that it urged him to cherish the days he had and was grateful for them.

He continued by saying that songs become associated with people and places and that a song's melody is a memory that can bring someone back, with their faces in full view as well. Introducing "One Tree Hill" as a song belonging to Carroll, Bono told the audience he knew that they probably have a similar story of a loved one passing away too early. [U2, Rome concert] On the projection screen during performances of "One Tree Hill" during The Joshua Tree Tour 2017, a red moon appeared alongside black-and-white footage of American Indians in the California desert. By the end of the song, the red moon illuminated the scenery and the desert was cascaded in red hues. Two American Indians, a man and a woman, appeared in indigenous attire as Bono, somberly, delivers the song's coda.

With the song's references to Victor Jara, Bono's introduction changed when U2 performed "One Tree Hill" in Santiago, Chile, during the final leg of The Joshua Tree Tour 2017. Instead of a remembrance of Carroll and the loved ones of those in the audience, Bono highlighted the political elements of the song, dedicating it to Jara and "those who fought injustice and who paid the highest price, even in this building," referring to the Estadio Nacional, the venue U2 was performing in where, four decades prior, dissidents who opposed Pinochet were tortured and murdered.

"One Tree Hill" is a remarkable song about endurance, loss, and love. It perfectly encapsulates one of the most important aspects of any journey, the need to brave adversity and the wisdom gained from overcoming it. With the underlying themes of journeying and discovery throughout *The Joshua Tree*, "One Tree Hill" adds a depth and richness that exemplifies the preciousness that is the gift of life. It is a treasure that we carry with ourselves and give to the meaningful people around us, however they come into our lives.

Chapter Fourteen

A Musical Journey

Identity is shaped by one's own personal journey. As we each move through our lives, gaining new experiences and scars along the way, we become more familiar with the essence of our being. New elements of perspective and insight are gained that reveal to us just how we perceive ourselves in the world, how others fit us into it, and offer us the wisdom of hindsight as we stop to see where we currently are and look back at how far our footsteps have taken us, reflecting on how we have evolved along the way. When we are born, we cannot escape having an identity. From day one, we are assigned a label that reflects a current social and cultural identity structure. We exist as a categorization of something as it relates to society as a whole. From then on, our experiences and the lessons we take from them allow us the autonomy to think more critically about ourselves and how we fit into a world that is constantly shaping us. The identity we begin life with is not the same one we take with us the rest of the way as part of our own personal journey. One in which our experiences allow us to shape our identity and its relationship to ourselves and the world around us.

By the end of Donald Trump's term as president, my relationship with my identity had shifted many times over the years. My understanding and connection with how I see myself, and how others see me, is vastly different now than when Trump took his oath of office. It is with these experiences, and many others throughout my life, that have given me the understanding and perception I have now about my identity.

An identity is really a reflection of one's own sense of self. It is a culmination of many different thoughts and experiences that clash or complement each other. And when that identity shifts, so does that version of the self, and we continue our journey to where this new version of our identity leads us. It is an endless journey, one where we may never find what we are looking for but it is the experiences we have along the way that bring us closer to a more complete actualization of self.

U2 and their existential journey through America recording *The Joshua Tree* inspired me to think intently about my own identity. The lessons I gained from their album provided me with insight about the troubling feelings I was having about my own American identity. Prior to discovering the album, I only had vague ideas about what my concerns were and how to express myself. It was through spending time with *The Joshua Tree*, and revealing the depth of its layers of commentary about the American Dream, that I started to make sense of my own experiences and how they had, and continue to have, shaped my life and identity. Every time I listened, I was joining the band as a fellow pilgrim seeking resolve in a country that failed to live up to its own promises at the expense of so many who had fallen into the gap of its ever-widening rift. The lessons U2 gained about America would set me on my own journey to understanding my American identity.

I was born in Texas in 1987, the same year *The Joshua Tree* was released, to an American father and an Irish mother. Having spent the vast majority of my life living in the United States, I was an American purely for the reason of having been born in the United States naturally. Growing up, there was not much more to think about my identity as an American other than it happened as a result of chance. As a child, your ability to think critically and introspectively about this has yet to mature and a nationality as an identity just happens to become something you accept and do not think about or challenge.

When the September 11th attacks were carried out in 2001, I was 13 years old and living in Alaska. As I would later come to understand, the attacks would be my first experience with collective trauma. It was the first event during my lifetime where I had some semblance of awareness of the impact it had on society in America and the reverberating effects it had on the rest of the world. It was a tragedy that opened my eyes to larger issues beyond the worldview I had developed up to that point. For the first time in my life, I had to think about what it meant to be an American and my relationship to the rest of the country.

Alaska, for me prior to September 11th, had always been a place that seemed like it was not really part of America. Not only is it so geographically removed from the contiguous United States, where people in the Lower 48 could easily travel between states without crossing through international borders, but it felt culturally different. The geography of Alaska in relation to the rest of the country instilled a more independent spirit and culture, almost as if it were a different country altogether. September 11th changed that. Regardless of the boundaries and geography, there was a shared identity that had been thrust on me.

Much like many others around the United States, since I was still just a budding teenager learning to understand who exactly I was and wanted to be, I was swept up in the patriotic fervor of the post-September 11th era that furthered an increasingly hardening and entrenched idea of what it was to be an American. With much of the country united, and supported by the nation's foreign allies, America's response to the attacks symbolized hope and resilience for several generations of Americans, many of whom who had not experienced a domestic attack from a foreign threat during their lifetimes.

During the early days in America's recovery, paeans to America's own sense of greatness were everywhere. In those days, it was considered uncouth to not outwardly display patriotism. Images of the American flag were everywhere, emblazoned on tchotchkes in all the stores and on commemorative keepsakes advertised on television at all hours and airing seemingly endlessly. The television and newspapers were filled with people wearing flag pins on their lapels. As a growing teenager, also swept up in the excitement of this new patriotic solidarity movement, I proudly wore my Old Navy flag shirts and joined in the chorus of tracking down the terrorists responsible and making them pay for their atrocities. It was a terrifying and exciting time and, at that age, I felt like I was part of something bigger than myself.

America changed immeasurably that day in many ways. Among those changes were those that either reinforced or challenged the preconceived notions many Americans had about their own national identity, including the idea of America as a land of rights that were inalienable and where opportunities were nearly guaranteed through the security of the country. For many, there were questions about why and how September 11th happened, with those struggling to overcome their own incredulousness of how something like that could happen in a country that proposed ideals such as equality and freedom. I, too, would be among those with complicated emotions I had yet to reckon with because of the lasting sting still being felt by this collective trauma. Although, I had something that would help me understand my emotions and provide an outlet for me to reconcile and make sense of them: a band I discovered almost a year before.

U2's tenth studio album *All That You Can't Leave Behind* was released on October 30, 2000, and its lead single "Beautiful Day" was an absolute jam. I am unsure if I had been aware of U2's music prior, let alone even heard of them to begin with, but none of that mattered. Whenever "Beautiful Day" came on the radio, my being was transcended. The song was big, anthemic, and brimming with a cool hook and melody that championed a spirit of unabashed optimism that I found so energizing.

And the album's follow-up singles kept me coming back for more with the synthesized chunkiness of "Elevation" and the emotional poignancy of "Walk On," with me trying to catch the music videos on VH1 or MTV in the morning before going to school. As a teenager, it was the first time I really connected with music on such a deeply emotional level. It did not matter whether I knew this was already an established rock band with career triumphs before I was even born, it was still music that excited me, allowed me to understand my explosively driven hormonal emotions and think about larger and more complex human ideas. Plus, it helped I could rock out to it.

During the summer of 2001, I went on a trip with my mother and sister to Ireland to visit my grandparents. I have no memories of any previous visits, so this was a thrilling opportunity for a 13-year-old. Unfortunately, I did not use this as an opportunity to spend time with family as a means of understanding my own heritage because such ideas were beyond the scope of my understanding and, most likely, interests at the time. For me, I was just excited I was in a different country. At 13, that meant seeing what their houses looked like, how different their candy bars were from the ones back home, and marveling at the fact I could see topless women in their tabloid newspapers, of which I tried to smuggle back home an issue or two in my luggage unbeknownst to my parents. The heritage connection did not seem so important. After all, I had an Irish parent and I saw evidence of that in my household growing up.

In retrospect, although my trip was a missed opportunity to explore my own history in a way I would be more inclined to do when I got older, it still planted its seed. In the city of Waterford, where my grandparents lived, I took a walk to a local music shop to see how different music was in Ireland compared with America. While I would find the music to be largely the same as what I could get back home, it was still interesting to browse. In that store, I picked up a copy of *All That You Can't Leave Behind*. Despite loving the songs whenever they came on the radio, I still did not own a copy of the album. Like most kids that age, I was not adept at saving money. However, I had an Irish pound note burning a hole in my pocket (euros had not been introduced in Ireland yet) that my grandmother had given me. For some reason I did not know, the Irish version of the CD had an extra track. That seemed pretty special and I bought it as my souvenir from my trip, a copy that I still own twenty years later.

Later in the year, after September 11th happened, and the United States increasingly became fanatical about its patriotism, I would see more of U2. Just 10 days after the attacks, the *America: A Tribute to Heroes* benefit concert was held to raise money for the victims of the attacks, their families, and the first responders who worked tirelessly among the wreckage. During that concert, U2, joined by Dave Stewart, Natalie Imbruglia, and Morleigh Steinberg, performed a version of "Walk On" with an intro featuring "Peace on Earth," another track from *All That You Can't Leave Behind.*

A few months later, on February 3, 2002, U2 performed during the halftime show at Super Bowl XXXVI. With this being the first major television broadcast of an American tradition that existed prior to September 11th, the stakes were incredibly high for the band. They had the responsibility to assuage America's collective grief with their music. The whole world would be watching to see how U2, a historically politically engaged band, would address the attacks, if at all. I remember watching and being incredibly moved by the performance. Following a performance of "Beautiful Day" that kicked off the show, a move to energize the fans watching the high-stakes sporting event with their recent big hit, the mood shifted to be more somber as U2 transitioned to "MLK." With Bono singing his tribute to Dr. Martin Luther King Jr., a somber prayer to the iconic figure of peace, a vertical scrim lowered and began scrolling the names of the victims of the attacks and continued while the band segued into "Where the Streets Have No Name" to elevate everyone's spirits once again before the game continued. I was then unaware of the meaning behind "Where the Streets Have No Name" and its narrative of yearning for a place where humanity's divisions were not demarcated, but I was moved by the spirit and emotional energy of the song during the performance. And when the performance was over and Bono, an Irishman, opened his jacket to reveal the American flag lining, a symbolic act of solidarity, I found myself intrigued. I could not explain why, but this felt a lot different than the flag-themed clothing I had seen the last few months, which were really indicative of a capitalist drive to profit off a tragedy. Looking back, this was likely the first time I had become aware of the fluidity of one's own identity and the experiences that shape us.

The dust of the shocking images of the World Trade Center's Ground Zero, permanently etched into our collective consciousness, seemed to settle as the patriotic unity that followed the aftermath of the attacks was soon replaced by a driving thirst for revenge and bloodshed. I was finishing my freshman year of high school when the US-led coalition invaded Iraq to overthrow Saddam Hussein in 2003, sparking the Iraq War that would continue officially for another eight years while also destabilizing the Middle East and resulting in various ongoing conflicts that still reverberate today. I was in the midst of my formative years and still figuring out how to eloquently communicate my thoughts and ideas on the conflict and my role as an American during it. The patriotic togetherness I had witnessed, and participated in, during the aftermath of the September 11th attacks had dissipated and the country was polarized between two factions: those who supported the war and those who opposed it. While I was in school learning about America's troubled history and various periods when the nation was divided on key issues, the Iraq War was the first instance during my lifetime that I witnessed America's inherent dichotomy and the disastrous effects of it in real time.

The war raging in Iraq was wrong. That much I felt to be true. The bombings and missile strikes, often impacting innocent civilians either wrongfully accused to have been insurgents or who were just casualties caught in the crossfire, were visually striking and disturbing as they played around-the-clock on cable news. Seeing families, women, and children covered in blood and dust, crying and severely injured, left an indelible impression on me as did the changing narrative and focus surrounding the war. The aftermath of the September 11th attacks contained a national rhetoric that preached unity and a collective idea of what it meant to be an American. As the bullets flew over the desert sands in Iraq, the rhetoric had shifted. The initial patriotic unity of our national dialogue fell out of style in favor of a more subtle form of racism that would eventually blow up to overt and pronounced Islamophobia.

The political discourse over the Iraq War carried out in the Capitol building in Washington, DC, and regurgitated in the media was the first time I became aware of America's inherent dichotomy. It was the effects of that discourse that echoed around the country and had a severely negative impact on Muslim Americans that really opened up my eyes to the idea that the country's dichotomy was growing. The impact the Iraq War had on Muslim Americans, and other people of color descending from the Middle East, was often violent and sometimes deadly. Hate crimes committed by nationalists and white supremacists during this time were becoming a regular occurrence. Assaults were frequent and more heinous acts like murder and the bombings of mosques were happening at an increasingly alarming rate. While each of these attacks against Muslims was often dismissed by many Americans as the act of a crazed lone wolf, America was failing to reckon with the growing Islamophobic and racist fires that were being stoked. In ways far less extreme than these hate crimes, though still rooting itself in America's systems, it became a point of pride for many people to proclaim they were anti-Muslim as a means of reinforcing their image of what an American identity should be. And for the first time in my life, my notion of what it meant to be an American was challenged. I viewed these Islamophobes as un-American much in the same way they viewed my humanism as un-American, albeit for different reasons. At that time with my understanding then, anyone who wanted a chance to achieve their own version of the American Dream was an American and was free to express that however they wished so as long as it did not impact the lives and freedoms of others. At first, I thought this putrid vitriol was because of a maligned belief that one had to be born in this country to be an American. It had never occurred to me before that I could be viewed as not an American, as not an equal, by others born in the same country as me, over ideological differences. I was still a child trying to figure all this out, but what I was finding was an increasingly disturbing realization that the idea of unity sold to me during my first experience with collective trauma was built on a lie. The divisions in America were widening before my eyes.

Several years later, when I was in college, the Islamophobic and anti-Muslim rhetoric grew to become part of the national dialogue during Barack Obama's first presidential campaign. As Obama advanced throughout the campaign toward securing the Democratic National Convention's party nomination, so did racist claims about his eligibility for the office. The birther movement, a conspiracy theory falsely asserting that Obama was not a natural-born citizen, relied on Islamophobic, anti-Muslim, and white supremacist beliefs espoused by those who were incredulous at the idea of a Black American becoming president. Despite all the evidence that supported the fact Obama was a natural-born citizen and, therefore, eligible for the presidency, it did not matter to the racist nationalists and white supremacists who championed their toxic politics. It was astounding to me to see an American like Obama denounced as being anything other than what he actually was on the basis of his skin color and family heritage. This was not an accusation that white presidential candidates were subjected to. I had already seen examples of American citizens claiming other citizens as not being American, but this was the first time the nation had seen a presidential candidate for a major political party defend their citizenship against a voter base containing an increasingly emboldened white supremacist faction. The idea of a group denouncing another American's legitimacy was now being normalized on a national scale and I was incredulous at how much further the country's dichotomous rift could open. It was appalling, and I was losing my faith in the idea that America could live up to its promises and alleged principles. I wanted to run and hide and hold on to something deeply rooted and stable. I sought guidance for anything that would help me reconcile my complex and shifting ideas about America. I needed to know if I could still appreciate America and my identity as an American while urging it to be better for everyone regardless of their racial and ethnic background. Little did I know that I would find my answer in a record shop, once again guided by the power of music.

It was during Obama's campaign in 2008, when I was 20, that I bought a used CD of *The Joshua Tree* at a local record store. I had previously only known the big hits from the album, but I was making more money from my part-time college job at a public radio station and I wanted to pick it up because it was often considered to be their best album. During this time, I was also heavily active with the campus student radio station, living and breathing that late-night disc jockey life. Although it was a place that exposed me to all kinds of wonderful new sounds, artists, and genres, they never did replace those first bands that I came to love and appreciate; U2 was one of them. *The Joshua Tree* was not the first album I purchased and admired deeply, but it was the first time when listening to an album gave me a much broader and more enlightened view of the world around me. Of course, other albums I had before were powerful and emotionally resonated with me, but none had challenged my perceptions of my own identity the way *The Joshua Tree* did.

The Joshua Tree really made me aware of the fluctuating concept of one's identity and relationship to it, and specifically, how strongly one felt connected to it as well as their ability to alter it to reflect their current worldview. Seeing Bono's jacket during the 2002 Super Bowl Halftime show was a curious thing for me at the time, but now through my more intimate understanding of the themes within *The Joshua Tree*, I started appreciating the deeper significance of Bono's expression. It was not just a show of solidarity to a nation that was still healing, but it represented Bono's, as well as the other members of U2's, relationship with America. It revealed to them facets of their own personal and cultural identities. New ideas and understanding about the challenges posed by the hypocrisy and alienation of America's policies. Challenges that could be overcome to make America an idea, as they believed, that belongs to people who need it the most. This enduring optimism was inspiring and I wanted to find a way to experience and share that. I wondered if I, too, could understand my own cultural identity by exploring that of another.

It was during the run up to the 2012 presidential election cycle that I started to think more deeply about the messaging of U2's music. As Obama ran for reelection, until ultimately facing Mitt Romney as the GOP nominee, the election cycle seemed more toxic and vitriolic than it had before. The 2012 presidential election was proving, through manipulation and misinformation from GOP leadership led by Senator Mitch McConnell, to be a referendum on Obama, one that was fueled by racism against America's first Black president and the Great Recession that he inherited from the previous administration.

Recently out of college and fresh to the city of Chicago, it was the first election that I remembered being politically engaged in. It was a dramatic time. Occupy Wall Street marches were happening all over the country, people were still recovering from the subprime mortgage crisis in which the big banks were bailed out, and there were escalating tensions with foreign leaders such as Mahmoud Ahmadinejad of Iran and Bashar al-Assad of Syria. I had not lived in a major city before, let alone any city that was so active in political demonstrations. All of my political engagement prior to moving to Chicago involved just chatting and discussing issues with friends over beers in my small college town. Now, I could actively engage on a level that was motivating and challenging, providing me with new experiences to shape my worldview and adopt ideals that reflected that.

It was during this time that I was listening to U2 more intently, with more concentration on the messaging, and finding a whole new appreciation for the band. The rhetoric of the 2012 election cycle was vitriolic and hateful as the political right, fueled by extremists and nationalists such as the grassroots Tea Party, adopted a more racist and hyperbolic outlook of America led by Obama. This sea change in American politics included Donald Trump, as the now de facto leader of the birther movement, and him continuing to question Obama's eligibility for president. Despite the evidence to disprove this conspiracy theory, including Obama releasing his official long-form birth certificate, the seed was already planted in the minds of the extremist right to continue channeling their racist vitriol against the president just for the color of his skin.

Amid all this awful rhetoric, America was taking a dark turn that forced me to question my role and responsibility as an American and whether the nation could endure through this division. I turned to U2's music for answers and to seek mental balance. Their music instilled in me an appreciation for humanism, and to look across the artifices that divide Americans. Their music rejected the notions of fanaticism and fundamentalism, things that I would see all over the news, while still advocating that there was still something to be hopeful for. When I read the news and felt hopeless, U2 showed me that America did not have to be that way. That America could, in fact, live up to the idea, as Bono has suggested, to be an idea for people who need it most.

Over the years, I returned to *The Joshua Tree* and found new layers of depth and meaning that helped me make sense of what was happening in the United States. Listening to U2's existential journey through America exploring their own identities, I started to reflect a lot more about my own. In *The Joshua Tree*, U2 sought to reconcile their complex emotions over their perception of America growing up in Ireland with the reality they discovered that the promised land was not even a promise but rather an illusion. Their understanding of the American Dream, what it meant for Americans as well as those who sought refuge within it, revealed their naivete as their eyes were open to the hypocrisies and destruction of America's political and wealthy elites. However, U2 also discovered for themselves that there was still much to love about America. Through their experiences with the music, literature, and culture of America, U2 also discovered that you could still admire much about a place that you also admonished. This reflected my own feelings about my country and my role in it, but I also found myself drawn to other aspects of my identity beyond my feeling of being an American and what that meant. U2's exploration of America allowed them to understand their own Irishness in a way they had never considered before. By the end of their journey, they would champion the idealized version of America they had grown up with and challenge the notion that America could not live up to the promise it shares. That realization was so insightful to me and it motivated me to find ways to reckon with these complex feelings. Much like the band did when recording *The Joshua Tree*, the album inspired me to understand my relationship to my own identity. Although I had never thought much about my own Irish background, I felt that getting Irish citizenship could help me understand my own Americanness and whether the country I had grown up in could become the shining beacon it had always claimed to be.

My connection to U2 was growing stronger, and it just felt like the right time to get my Irish citizenship and to officially share a cultural identity with the band. *The Joshua Tree* played a significant role in that, shaping my understanding of the flaws America had always suffered from, but that there still is a need to strive for the ideals that the concept of America had represented to generations before me. Turning on the news and feeling dismal about the country's future seemed so prevalent, with viewers committing to some perverse form of self-flagellation watching the violence and hate speech unfold on the screen in real-time and lamenting over whether anything could stop this. It was easy to get depressed and feel suffocated by the miasma of the 24/7 news cycle. I knew things were not going well, but it did not change the fact that things could be made right and the country's dichotomy closed. U2 was making me an optimist at a time when it was not hip to be one, and I questioned my identity as a result of it. I started to feel less like an American because so many with nationalist and racist beliefs were asserting I was not one.

I started to pursue the Irish citizenship application process in 2011, just before the 2012 election cycle came into full swing. It took several years before I got all of the documents together for my application. For one, every document I needed cost money and, at that time, I did not have much to put into the application. It took time to save and get every piece of paper, one by one, that I needed for the application. For me to get the citizenship, I had to apply through Foreign Births Registration, meaning that I could be an Irish citizen on the basis that my grandparents were Irish. I just needed all the proper paperwork connecting me to them.

To get my citizenship, I was not the only one going on a journey exploring cultural identity. My mother was born in England but was adopted by an Irish couple. Unfortunately, during the time I was working on my citizenship application, her parents were dealing with significant health issues, and it did not feel right to burden them with finding various documents they may not have had. So, my mother set out to find the identity of her biological parents, obtaining necessary paperwork and documentation that I would then use for my citizenship application. Finding her birth parents, ultimately an Irish couple, took my mom a few years and was not an easy journey, emotionally or otherwise, but it did serve a purpose of giving her closure after being put up for adoption five decades prior.

In a world where everyone has a story to tell and is walking the path of their journey, we tend to cross paths with others and our respective journeys are impacted as a result. For me to complete my journey of getting citizenship, my mother had to finish her own. Without her need to find the identity of her birth parents, getting the documents I needed would have been more difficult, too overwhelming, and I likely would not have further connected myself with U2 and their music in a way that I felt necessary. All of our individual problems are, in ways large or small, connected with the problems of others. That is an underlying theme in *The Joshua Tree*: all Americans facing a struggle that can be alleviated when people unite. I know it might seem disingenuous to talk about my mother helping me get Irish citizenship and equating it to songs about the band condemning military intervention in foreign lands or analyzing the deranged mind of those left behind on the fringes of the American wasteland, but that is not the point. The point is that we all, in a multitude of ways, rely on each other to reach an actualization of ourselves, as both individuals and as members of society. Otherwise, we contribute to the rift in the American dichotomy, this difference between the reality and mythos perpetuated by those in power, and that does not help us live better as people or as Americans. This would prove to be something I became increasingly cognizant of as America marched toward an existential crisis.

It was the middle of 2016 by the time I sent off my application for Irish citizenship to the General Consulate of Ireland in Chicago. By the time I did that, Donald Trump was close to defeating his last two primary opponents, out of an initial 17 in 2015, to secure the Republican nomination for president. The 2012 election cycle was bad, but it was nothing like the 2016 campaign. Since enabling a base of loyal followers with his birther claims in 2012, Trump was becoming more popular in mainstream conservatism. Over the course of his campaign, he dialed up the nationalist and white supremacist rhetoric and adopted an authoritarian outlook for his vision of America. Declaring the press as the enemy of the people, threatening to ban certain types of immigrants, and even inciting violence at his rallies, he was laying the groundwork for the white ethno state of America he envisioned and which excited and emboldened extremists among his supporters.

With every election cycle, there is always that trope of the disheartened voter threatening to leave the country if their candidate's opponent wins. You would hear that in every election cycle, but it really came out in full effect in 2016.

I shared updates with friends and family about my citizenship application progress over the course of the campaign. As November 2016 drew near and Trump was ascending the ranks of the Republican party toward a nomination, people joked that I needed to leave the United States as soon as my citizenship was approved; that this was my chance to get out of a country that was on a march toward self-destruction. My original goal of obtaining Irish citizenship was not to leave the United States permanently, but the concept of a Trump presidency made me seriously consider that option for the first time. I recognized the inherent privilege of being able to escape a sinking ship at the first sign of trouble. This thought was not comforting, and I struggled to make sense of how one man, Trump, could shape my journey and motivations behind it. Just as U2 became aware of the divide that created a dichotomous America while recording *The Joshua Tree*, I was witnessing the widening of the country's cultural and social gaps.

By February 2017, weeks after Trump spoke about American carnage at his presidential inauguration, I received confirmation that I was now a dual citizen with the United States and the Republic of Ireland. Admittedly, it was rather bittersweet. I had not expected Trump to win the election, and I recalled all the conversations I had with friends leading up to this moment about how I now had a golden ticket to escape the devastation many expected Trump to cause.

The world after Trump's inauguration seemed so far removed from the one when I first set out to obtain Irish citizenship. Much like how differently U2 saw America before and after recording *The Joshua Tree* as it related to their Irish identity, so now did my relationship with my own American identity change after I had citizenship in another country. And not just any country, but the same one where U2 was from. This was not a superficial detail to me in the slightest. It was a manifestation of this idea I had about my own country and the nuance of speaking truth to power to something that is a part of you and something that has shaped you. I have had great experiences in America, albeit for reasons that were due to my privilege as a white man, an experience that could not be shared on the same level by many women, people of color, or other marginalized groups that are adversely affected by the policies that aim to widen, or at least maintain, the dichotomy of America.

U2's existential journey gave voice to my own journey in understanding my own identity. Much in the same way America revealed to them the many facets of their own Irishness, so did their Irishness reveal to me a complexity of my own Americanness: mainly that it is acceptable to criticize something that I love and is a part of me, while still yearning and advocating for it to live up to its most idyllic self—a sense of self that stands to unify everyone and bring out the best of ourselves and not have us devolve into American carnage. This instilled in me a belief that every American has an inherent responsibility to reconcile the nation's cultural and social gaps, and to do that requires not just exclusively examining and denouncing the nation's most destructive qualities but elevating those that are positive and worth championing as well. Otherwise, if there was never anything worth celebrating in America to begin with, then what is even the point of striving toward what the idealized vision of America could be? There is not any. To fail one group is to fail all.

During the days after getting my citizenship confirmation, all the conversations I had with friends about my alleged golden ticket came flooding back to me. The unexpected had happened with the election results, and I was feeling more uneasy than ever about my identity. I had the passport and all the documents that gave me the power to leave, but it did not seem so easy. Since Trump won the election, America experienced an increasingly emboldened level of perverse nationalism and white supremacy that previously existed, in modern times, but were less obvious and typically among the fringes of the culture. Travel bans against Muslims, quid pro quos with foreign leaders to investigate political opponents, complicity in the murder of unarmed Black men and women by police, the intentional downplaying of a global pandemic for political gain, and impeachment for inciting an insurrection not only defined Trump and his desire for an actualization of a national and authoritarian white ethno state, but these events furthered the widening of the dichotomous rift that existed within the country and among its people. Even a few years after acquiring my Irish citizenship to better understand my own American identity, I continue to be challenged as I reconcile with my own feelings.

One of the biggest lessons I have learned from this is that while the destination may seem impossible, it is the journey and what we do on it that truly matters. Though U2's vision of America had changed and grown more complex, they still had not found what they were looking for—and neither have I. The constant threats to democracy and people's overall health and safety were continuously at risk under Trump, and dealing with the deluge of his policies became ever increasingly exhausting and worrisome. Trump's vision of America was not the same one I, and millions of others, have for this country. The easy solution is to just run away, but there is no satisfaction in that. The hard work in achieving the promise of the American Dream for everyone comes from the demonstrations and protests that have challenged Trump since before he sat in the Oval Office, as well as the reverberations of his influence since leaving. And the work is hard because the reward is great. The reason why people stand up to authoritarians and demagogues is that they have a vision for their country that represents a refuge for all. It is not easy to achieve, but it is something of value worth fighting for. U2 recognized that with their experiences through America recording *The Joshua Tree*, I recognized that through my experiences and the lessons from the album, and millions of others recognize that when they continue to turn human wrongs into human rights. I could not let Trump define my identity as an American by critiquing the country from afar. To have America reflect the change I want to see means to stand up and fight alongside those who stand to risk far more than I stand to lose.

U2 knew the idea of what America represented to them in Ireland was one worth fighting to maintain. I reasoned that the ability to leave the United States is indicative of privilege that not many Americans have, and anyone who has that privilege likely has a better quality of life than those who do not. In other words, people most threatened by Trump's policies would be even worse off. This was a reason to stay behind and fight to create an America where all are truly free—a lesson U2 had learned and shared three decades previously through *The Joshua Tree*. And much like the temptation U2 encountered recording *The Joshua Tree*, so I continue to reckon with my own temptations to leave. If I were ever to leave the country, it would have to be for far greater and more personal reasons than just merely escaping Trump and his legacy.

U2 were all in their mid-20s when they recorded *The Joshua Tree* and released it the year I was born. Coincidentally, I was also in my mid-

20s when I pursued Irish citizenship during a tempestuous political era that ushered in an extremist version of the politics U2 criticized on *The Joshua Tree*. Through U2's music and messages on that album, I discovered something new within myself. What started as a love for the band and a fascination with their Irish background eventually turned into an intimate understanding of a sacred message they shared as a result of their own journey. I realized that apathy is the death of the mythic idea of America. If we truly believed in what this country could achieve, we could not be blind to the reality of its flaws and would have to work together to uphold the value of the American mythos.

My journey to Irish citizenship as seen through the lens of America's changing political climate is how I realized the themes of *The Joshua Tree* were relevant in a modern context. The band's and album's messages were never meant to disparage America. The truths told on the record and on stage, both in 1987 and 2017, were meant to encourage America and that the ideals America represented to U2 growing up in Ireland in the 1970s were worth the struggle. Though they discovered a dichotomy within America, U2 never gave up on the idea that the American Dream is a dream we can and must all share.

Epilogue

The Joshua Tree

Barreling down a stretch of desert highway west of Death Valley, the sun at its peak raining rays of hellfire on my rental car, I was on a pilgrimage. Alone for miles, not having seen another car or person for almost an hour, I felt a wave of freedom fall over me as I left nothing behind me but a trail of dust. I had come too far to turn around. No, I would not stop until I found what I was looking for.

Arriving at my destination several hours after my plane landed, I finally pulled over to the side of the highway and with a feeling of such isolation that I probably could have just parked in the middle of the road and had no issues. I got out of the car, went to the trunk, and took generous gulps of water from the jug I kept back there in case I was stranded. I was in the hottest and driest part of the country after all—a place no one goes to unless they have a reason.

As I was drinking my water, I leaned against the car and stared down the highway in the direction I had just come from. I had come a long way to be here, enjoying my water and its life-giving essence that is so scarce in this part of America that I had suddenly felt like the richest man in the world. I stared off into the distance at where the road met the horizon and thought about the journey I took to get here. All the stretches of desert highways and winding canyon roads through the harshest climate I had ever seen. It left me feeling so alive.

Finished with my water, I closed the trunk and stared off to the side of the highway into the California desert. This would be the last leg of my journey—one I had ventured on alone. I was looking for something out there, something that had to be seen to be believed.

After tightening my boots, I set out putting rubber to sand. I did not have far to travel, but every step I made was conscious and deliberate. I was a stranger in this land, and I had no desire to disrupt the balance that was around me. Though I had not seen another person for a while, I was not truly alone. The desert was teeming with life, even after death. For me, this was hallowed ground.

In the distance, a mass was taking shape. The sun was blinding, but I could see something manifesting before me, growing bigger with every step I took. I could not quite make out its features yet, but it seemed to even change shape. My mind was either playing tricks on me or I could not believe what I was seeing. Soon, I was close enough to know that I found what I was looking for.

Laying there in the desert sand was a Joshua tree. Or more specifically, *the* Joshua tree. The one that appears with U2 on the album that is its namesake. Once gloriously reaching into the heavens when U2 stumbled on it during their existential journey through America, it now lay on the ground after living a full and storied life.

Surrounding the tree were relics left by other pilgrims who had made this same journey over the years. Guitars, placards, flags, and canisters of various sizes surrounded this spiritual and musical icon. Around the area were rocks and stones reorganized to create messages or symbols, U2 hieroglyphics that only fans would know. Though, I supposed someone who did not appreciate their music likely would not have been here anyway. There was nothing else, no other reason, for being here.

It was March 2019 and I had just finished the first draft of this book. As a reward for hitting that milestone, I felt a much-needed vacation was in order and I had decided to find this Joshua tree as a way to celebrate. It was a trip that sort of brought me full circle. This tree represented a work of art that challenged me to think about my own identity as I wrote a book about a group who made that art to explore their own identities. I did not know what to expect, or what I would think about, when I found this tree. I tried to leave myself open to where the spirit of this tree would take me.

I walked slowly around the tree adorned with the items of admiration left by fans over the years. As I kneeled down to look at some of the inscriptions on the items, opened containers to browse through letters and photos, and the other ways previous travelers left their mark, I was experiencing several complicated feelings.

I thought a lot about America and what had brought me to this spot at this moment. So much had already happened under the Trump administration. Foreign influence in the election. Muslim bans. Challenging North Korea with nuclear devastation. Children locked in cages along the border. Emboldened white supremacists marching with torches. So much had already happened to shift America in the direction of an authoritarian state in just a few short years. Standing there, I could not imagine what would come next. Major civil and social unrest over racial justice and a global pandemic were only a year away, catalysts for the ending of Trump's presidency and the resulting incitement of an insurrectionist siege on the US Capitol provoked by Trump's Big Lie about losing the election in the waning weeks of his presidency. Though at that time it was difficult to imagine what events would unfold during the remainder of Trump's presidency, looking back, I am a bit envious of the naivete I had standing over that tree.

The tree fell nearly two decades prior to my visit, but it looked as though it just had yesterday. Nothing seems to age or decay in the desert. Even in death, an energy radiated around this tree. I wonder if this represented how I felt about America at the time, that a spirit can live on even after the most dire of circumstances. U2 believed there was something of value in America to hold on to and championed that it was worth preserving, elevating, and sharing with everyone. Even during the most dismal days of the Trump presidency, when I would feel most conflicted about my identity and relationship with America, part of me still shared this value. This fallen tree still meant so much to those who sought it, and perhaps it also meant that America could still mean something for those who still believed in it. Or was this just a shrine to an idea that had been lost long before I showed up? Was it too late for me? Was it too late for anyone? These were the hard questions U2 asked themselves when they saw this tree alive and well, and the same ones I asked myself three decades later as I gazed at it sprawled on the desert floor.

Still reflecting on my thoughts and having more questions than I could answer for myself at that moment, I turned to leave. However, not far from the fallen tree, there was a plaque built into a cement block in the ground. Having turned various shades of green aged by the blazing desert sun and rough-hewn from the blowing sand over the years, the plaque featured an engraving of the very same Joshua tree laying near it but as it was depicted on its album namesake. Not far from where it had fallen, the tree had been given new life to represent a place where not only musical history was made but also where history would be made for all those listened to and loved *The Joshua Tree*.

Below the engraving of the tree, on the plaque asks the question "Have you found what you're looking for?" I stared at that question for several minutes, thinking about what it meant to me at that exact place at that exact moment. In one sense, I did. I had found the fallen tree I sought out. However, in another sense, I had the awareness to know that I had not. Finding the tree instilled in me so many questions about

my identity and what comes next for America. Gazing at the plaque and thinking deeply about the question it asked me, I felt a glimmer of hope. The same kind that I had felt when I first listened to *The Joshua Tree* and that had grown every time I did over the years. I looked up and stared back in the direction I had just come from, first at my car and then tracing the highway along the horizon. I took one last look at the plaque, then the tree, and then turned around and walked back to my car thinking that the America U2 and I hope for, an idea for people who desperately need it most of all, is still out there and waiting to be found.

References

Alan, Carter. 1992. *Outside Is America: U2 in the U.S.* Boston, MA: Faber & Faber.

Allen, Bob. 2017. "U2's Joshua Tree 2017 Tour Wraps with $316 Million Earned." *Billboard*, November 1. https://www.billboard.com/articles/columns/chart -beat/8022273/u2-the-joshua-tree-2017-tour-earnings.

Apple Music. 2017. "U2: Joshua Tree 30th Anniversary Interview | Apple Music." *YouTube*. https://www.youtube.com/watch?v=vsKZ3YrF_3Q.

Assayas, Michka. 2006. *Bono: In Conversation with Michka Assayas.* New York, NY: Riverhead Books.

Austin, David. 1990. "Longing, Obsession and an Actress' Death: Robert John Bardo Says His Infatuation with Rebecca Schaeffer Dominated His Life." *The Oregonian*, July 18.

Averill, Steve, ed. 1987. *The Joshua Tree Tour Programme.*

Barrón-López, Laura. 2020. Review of *Trump Attacks Take a Toll on Black Lives Matter Support. Politico*, September 2. https://www.politico.com/news/2020/09/02/trump-black-lives-matter-poll-407227.

BBC. "1984: The Beginning of the End for British Coal." http://news.bbc.co.uk/onthisday/hi/dates/stories/march/12/newsid_3503000/3503346.stm.

BBC. "The Miners' Strike." http://www.bbc.co.uk/wales/history/sites/themes/society/industry_coal06.shtml.

Beckwith, Karen. 1996. "Lancashire Women against Pit Closures: Women's Standing in a Men's Movement." *Signs* 21 (4): 1034–68.

Berger, Miriam. 2020. "Invaders, Allies, Occupiers, Guests: A Brief History of U.S. Military Involvement in Iraq." *The Washington Post*, January 11. https://www.washingtonpost.com/world/2020/01/11/invaders-allies-occupiers -guests-brief-history-us-military-involvement-iraq/.

Bhattacharjee, Riya. 2016. "'You're Fired'—Bono Breaks Down Trump's Wall at Bay Area U2 Benefit Concert." *NBC Bay Area*, October 9. https://

www.nbcbayarea.com/news/local/youre-fired-bono-breaks-down-trumps
-wall-at-u2-benefit-concert-in-sf/2065463/.

Black, Susan. 1996. *Bono in His Own Words*. London, UK: Omnibus Press.

Block, Adam. 1989. "Bono Bites Back." *Mother Jones*, May 1.

Bowler, Dave, and Bryan Dray. 1993. *U2: A Conspiracy of Hope*. London, UK: Pan Macmillan.

Bradshaw, John S. 1983. "Drug Misuse in Ireland, 1982–1983: Investigation in a North Central Dublin Area, and in Galway, Sligo and Cork." *Medico-Social Research Board* AA2, VH4.2. https://www.drugsandalcohol.ie/5060/1/321 -0263.pdf.

Breskin, David. 1987. "Interview with Bono." *Rolling Stone*, October 8.

Brothers, Robyn. 1999. "Time to Heal, 'Desire' Time." In *Reading Rock and Roll: Authenticity, Appropriation, Aesthetics*, edited by Kevin J. H. Dettmar, and William Richey, 237–67. New York, NY: Columbia University Press.

Chatterton, Mark. 2001. *U2: The Complete Encyclopedia*. London, UK: Firefly.

Christopher, Michael. 2017. "U2 Plunge Into Darkness on 'Exit': The Story Behind Every 'Joshua Tree' Song." *Diffuser.Fm* (blog). March 9. https://diffuser.fm/u2-exit/.

"CIA Activities in Chile—Central Intelligence Agency." 2013. Central Intelligence Agency. https://www.cia.gov/library/reports/general-reports-1/chile/ index.html#1.

Classic Albums: U2 The Joshua Tree. Directed by Philip King and Nuala O'Connor. Eagle Rock Entertainment, 1999.

Cocks, Jay. 1987. "U2: Band on the Run." *Time*, April 27.

Cogan, Višnja. 2008. *U2 : An Irish Phenomenon*. New York, NY: Pegasus Books.

Collins, Sean. 2020. "Trump Once Flirted with White Nationalism. Now It's a Centerpiece of His White House." *Vox*, July 21. https://www.vox .com/21313021/trump-white-nationalism-supremacy-miller-bannon -immigration.

Cordova, Cary. 2017. *The Heart of the Mission: Latino Art and Politics in San Francisco*. Philadelphia: University of Pennsylvania Press.

Daly, Rhian. 2017. "Bono Says 'Where The Streets Have No Name' Is 'Unfinished.'" *New Musical Express*, July 20. https://www.nme.com/news/music/ bono-unfinished-streets-name-2113648.

DeCurtis, Anthony. 1987. "U2: Truths and Consequences." *Rolling Stone*, May 7. https://www.rollingstone.com/music/music-features/u2-truths-and-conse quences-100017/.

DeRiso, Nick. 2017. "U2's 'Red Hill Mining Town' Explores Personal Costs in an Economic Downturn: The Story Behind Every 'Joshua Tree' Song." *Diffuser. Fm* (blog). March 5. https://diffuser.fm/u2-red-hill-mining-town/.

Detweiler, Craig, and Barry Taylor. 2003. *A Matrix of Meanings: Finding God in Pop Culture.* Grand Rapids, MI: Baker Academic.

Deutsch, Linda. 1991. "Obsessed Fan Convicted in Slaying of Actress Rebecca Schaeffer." *Associated Press,* October 29.

Diamond, Anna. 2018. "The Original Meanings of the 'American Dream' and 'America First' Were Starkly Different from How We Use Them Today." *Smithsonian Magazine,* December. https://www.smithsonianmag.com/history/behold-america-american-dream-slogan-book-sarah-churchwell-180970311/.

Doyle, Tom. 2017. "American Dreams." *Mojo,* April.

Dunphy, Eamon. 1987. *Unforgettable Fire: Past, Present and Future—The Definitive Biography of U2.* New York, NY: Warner.

Eccleston, Danny. 2017. "U2: Inside Their Joshua Tree Tour." *Mojo,* July 7. https://www.mojo4music.com/articles/25586/u2-inside-their-joshua-tree-tour.

Endrinal, Christopher. 2014. "Vocal Layering as Deconstruction and Reinvention in U2." In *Exploring U2: Is This Rock "n" Roll?: Essays on the Music, Work, and Influence of U2,* edited by Scott D. Calhoun, 67–83. Lanham, MD: Rowman & Littlefield.

Evans, Chris. 2017. *The Chris Evans Breakfast Show.* BBC Radio 2.

Fakazis, Liz. 2016. "New Journalism | American Literary Movement." In *Encyclopædia Britannica.* https://www.britannica.com/topic/New-Journalism.

Fallon, Jimmy. 2017. *The Tonight Show* NBC. September 7.

Galbraith, Deane. 2014. "Fallen Angels in the Hands of U2." In *Exploring U2: Is This Rock "n" Roll?: Essays on the Music, Work, and Influence of U2,* edited by Scott D. Calhoun. 179–94. Lanham, MD: Rowman & Littlefield.

Gallen, Joel, and Beth McCarthy. 2001. *America: A Tribute to Heroes.* Line by Line Productions. September 21.

Garrett, Greg. 2009. *We Get to Carry Each Other: The Gospel According to U2.* Louisville, KY: Westminster John Knox Press.

Garvey, Megan. 2016. "Bono: Trump Is 'Potentially the Worst Idea That Ever Happened to America.'" *Los Angeles Times,* September 20. https://www.latimes.com/nation/politics/trailguide/la-na-trailguide-updates-bono-trump-the-worst-idea-ever-for-1474377850-htmlstory.html.

"Gary Gilmore | Biography, Crimes, Execution, & Facts." n.d. *Encyclopedia Britannica.* https://www.britannica.com/biography/Gary-Gilmore.

Gilbert, Andrew. 2014. "Singing It Right Out Loud: How Protest Songs Have Propelled Progressive Politics." *California Magazine*, November 9. https://alumni.berkeley.edu/california-magazine/just-in/2014-11-09/singing-it -right-out-loud-how-protest-songs-have-propelled.

Goñi, Uki. 2017. "40 Years Later, the Mothers of Argentina's 'Disappeared' Refuse to Be Silent." *The Guardian*, April 17. https://www.theguardian.com/world/2017/apr/28/mothers-plaza-de-mayo-argentina-anniversary.

Goyette, Jared. 2015. "How the Forgotten Music of the Civil Rights Movement Was Hiding in Plain Sight." *The World*, April 14. https://www.pri.org/stories/2015-04-14/how-forgotten-music-civil-rights-movement-was-hiding-plain-sight.

Graham, Bill, and Niall Stokes. 1987. "U2 Gives Themselves Away." *Musician*, May.

Greene, Andy. 2014. "Readers' Poll: The 10 Best U2 Deep Cuts." *Rolling Stone*, September 17. https://www.rollingstone.com/music/music-lists/readers-poll -the-10-best-u2-deep-cuts-160922/trip-through-your-wires-164179/.

———. 2016. "Flashback: Bob Dylan Sings 'Blowin' in the Wind' with Bono." *Rolling Stone*, August 9. https://www.rollingstone.com/music/music-news/flashback-bob-dylan-sings-blowin-in-the-wind-with-bono-103281/.

———. 2017. "Bono on How U2's 'Songs of Experience' Evolved, Taking on Donald Trump." *Rolling Stone*, September 20. https://www.rollingstone.com/music/music-features/bono-on-how-u2s-songs-of-experience-evolved-taking-on-donald-trump-253312/.

———. 2017. "Bono Talks 'Joshua Tree' Tour, Trump, Status of U2's Next Album." *Rolling Stone*, May 30. https://www.rollingstone.com/music/music-features/bono-talks-joshua-tree-tour-trump-status-of-u2s-next-album-121562/.

———. 2017. "The Edge Breaks Down U2's Upcoming 'Joshua Tree' Tour." *Rolling Stone*, January 9. https://www.rollingstone.com/music/music-features/the -edge-breaks-down-u2s-upcoming-joshua-tree-tour-111050/.

———. 2017. "U2's Longtime Stage Designer Talks 'Joshua Tree' Tour 2017." *Rolling Stone*, January 26. https://www.rollingstone.com/music/music-features/u2s-longtime-stage-designer-talks-joshua-tree-tour-2017-128983/.

Halperin, Shirley. 2017. "Bono 'Hated the Singer': Producer Steve Lillywhite on Revisiting U2's 'Red Hill Mining Town.'" *Variety*, June 7. https://

variety.com/2017/music/news/u2-red-hill-mining-town-steve-lillywhite
-mix-1202456781/.

Happy Christmas. *U2.com* (blog). December 25, 2016.

Hastings, Rob. 2017. "'Exit': The Song U2 Dared Not Play after a Murderer
Blamed the Track for Him Killing a TV Actress." *Inews*, June 28. https://
inews.co.uk/culture/music/u2-exit-robert-john-bardo-murder-rebecca
-schaeffer-joshua-tree-2017-75364.

Higgins, Kate. 2015. "Women's Library@LSE Archive—Women and the Miners'
Strike." *The London School of Economic and Political Science* (blog). March.

Hilburn, Robert. 1987. "U2's Bono Hewson Pours Drama into Rock." *Chicago
Sun-Times*, December 25.

History.com Editors. 2018. "9/11 Attacks." History. December 12. https://www
.history.com/topics/21st-century/9-11-attacks.

Hot Press. 1986. "The U2 Covers: No. 12, 'The Edge Goes Solo.'" *Hot Press*. October 9.

———. 1988. "I Still Haven't Found What I'm Looking For." *Hot Press*. December 1.

———. 2017. "The U2 Covers: No. 41, 'Reach Out and Touch the Flame.'" *Hot
Press*, July 18. https://www.hotpress.com/culture/the-u2-covers-no-41
-reach-out-and-touch-the-flame-20387645.

Hughes, Hilary. 2017. "U2's Joshua Tree Tour Revisits the Band's Greatest Era—
But Its Urgency Has Faded Three Decades Later." *Esquire*, July 17. https://
www.esquire.com/entertainment/music/a56353/u2-joshua-tree-tour-review/.

Inskeep, Steve. 2017. "U2 On 'The Joshua Tree,' a Lasting Ode to a Divided
America." *Morning Edition.* National Public Radio. March 20. https://www
.npr.org/2017/03/20/520443744/u2-on-the-joshua-tree-a-lasting-ode-to-a
-divided-america.

Irwin, Colin. 1987. "This Is What We Do Best." *Melody Maker*, March 14.

Jackson, Joe. 1993. "Bono vs. The Beast." *Musician*, August.

Jobling, John. 2014. *U2: The Definitive Biography*. New York, NY: Thomas Dunne
Books.

Joseph, Peniel. 2016. "Obama's Effort to Heal Racial Divisions and Uplift Black
America." *The Washington Post*, April 22. https://www.washingtonpost.com/
graphics/national/obama-legacy/racism-during-presidency.html.

Kantas, Harry, and Aaron J. Sam. 2017. "Greg Carroll: The Heart of 'The Joshua Tree.'" *U2 Songs* (blog). June 9. https://www.u2songs.com/news/greg_car roll_the_heart_of_the_joshua_tree.

Kaye, Ben. 2017. "U2 Perform "I Still Haven't Found What I'm Looking For" on Kimmel, Accompanied by Gospel Choir—Watch." *Consequence of Sound* (blog). May 24. https://consequenceofsound.net/2017/05/u2-perform-i-still -havent-found-what-im-looking-for-on-kimmel-accompanied-by-gospel -choir-watch/.

Keuss, Jeffrey F., and Sara Koenig. 2014. "The Authentic Self in Paul Riceour and U2." In *Exploring U2: Is This Rock "n" Roll?: Essays on the Music, Work, and Influence of U2*, edited by Scott D. Calhoun 54–64. Lanham, MD: Rowman & Littlefield.

Kimmel, Jimmy. 2017. *Jimmy Kimmel Live*. ABC. May 23.

Kreps, Daniel. 2016. "Watch U2 Blast Donald Trump During 'Desire' at IHeart-Radio Festival." *Rolling Stone*, September 25. https://www.rollingstone.com/ music/music-news/watch-u2-blast-donald-trump-during-desire-at-iheart radio-festival-108479/.

Leas, Ryan. 2017. "U2 Return to 'The Joshua Tree' in Trump's America." *Stereo-gum*, June 30. https://www.stereogum.com/1949942/u2-returns-to-the -joshua-tree-in-trumps-america/concert/.

Lederman, Marsha. 2017. "Carefully Planned Chaos: A Look at How an Iconic Video Came Together 30 Years Ago." *The Globe and Mail*, May 9. https:// www.theglobeandmail.com/arts/music/u2s-where-the-streets-have-no -name-30-yearslater/article34932271/.

Lipshutz, Jason. 2016. "U2 Posts Christmas Message for Fans." *Billboard*, Decem-ber 25. https://www.billboard.com/articles/columns/rock/7633291/u2-2017 -tour.

Mangan, Dan. 2020. "Trump Suggests Lincoln's Legacy Is 'Questionable,' Brags about His Own Work for Black Americans." *CNBC*, June 12. https://www .cnbc.com/2020/06/12/trump-criticizes-lincoln-brags-he-has-done-a-lot -to-help-black-americans.html.

McCormick, Neil, and U2. 2006. *U2 by U2*. London, UK: HarperCollins.

McGee, Matt. 2008. *U2: A Diary*. London, UK: Omnibus.

———. 2017. "Bono Explains Why U2 Never Played 'Red Hill Mining Town' Live." *AtU2* (blog). April 20. https://www.atu2.com/news/bono-explains -why-u2-never-played-red-hill-mining-town-live.html.

———. 2017. "The @U2 Interview: Willie Williams Talks About The Joshua Tree Tour 2017." *AtU2* (blog). June 8. https://www.atu2.com/news/the-u2 -interview-willie-williams-talks-about-the-joshua-tree-tour-2017.html.

McPherson, Alan L. 2015. *The World and U2: One Band's Remaking of Global Activism*. Lanham, MD: Rowman & Littlefield.

"Miners' Strike 1984–1985—Archives Hub." 2010. Jisc.Ac.Uk. https://archives hub.jisc.ac.uk/features/mar04.shtml.

Mirkin, Steven. 2017. "Inside the Song: The Sustained Brilliance of U2's 'With or Without You.'" *Fender*. https://www.fender.com/articles/artists/one-track -mind-the-sustained-brilliance-of-u2s-with-or-without-you.

"Mr. Reagan's War on Poverty." *The New York Times*, October 2, 1981. https:// www.nytimes.com/1981/10/02/opinion/mr-reagan-s-war-on-poverty.html.

Musician. 1987. Review of *U2 Give Themselves Away*. *Musician*, May.

National Football League. 2002. *The Super Bowl XXXVI Halftime Show*. Fox. February 3.

Neufeld, Timothy D. 2017. *U2: Rock 'n' Roll to Change the World*. Lanham, MD: Rowman & Littlefield.

"New Movies: Anatomy of a Murder." *Time Magazine*, December 22, 1967. http:// content.time.com/time/magazine/article/0,9171,899952,00.html.

O'Hare, Colm. 2007. "The Secret History of 'The Joshua Tree.'" *Hot Press*, November 7. https://www.hotpress.com/music/the-secret-history-of-the-joshua -tree-4269254.

Pareles, Jon. 2017. "Review: U2 Revisits 'The Joshua Tree' in the Here and Now." *The New York Times*, May 15. https://www.nytimes.com/2017/05/15/arts/ music/u2-joshua-tree-30th-anniversary-tour-review.html.

Parkyn, Geoff. 1988. *U2 Touch the Flame: An Illustrated Documentary*. New York, NY: Perigee Books.

Patricia, Francis. 2018. "Review of 'We Are Women, We Are Strong': Celebrating the Unsung Heroines of the Miners' Strike." *The Conversation*, March 9. https://theconversation.com/we-are-women-we-are-strong-celebrating -the-unsung-heroines-of-the-miners-strike-92448.

PRI and WNYC. 2015. "Rediscovering the Hidden Music of the Civil Rights Movement." *Studio 360*, April 1.

Rascoe, Ayesha. 2020. Review of "Trump Campaign Trying to Win Over Black Voters, But President Remains a Tough Sell." *National Public Radio*, August

14. https://www.npr.org/2020/08/14/902236623/trump-campaign
-trying-to-win-over-black-voters-but-president-remains-a-tough-sel.

"Rene Castro & the Love Town '89 Sets." *Propaganda*, Issue 11, September 1, 1989.

Rietmulder, Michael. 2018. "Eddie Vedder Helps U2 Celebrate 'Joshua Tree' During Band's First U.S. Show in Trump Era." *Seattle Magazine*, November 27. https://www.seattlemag.com/arts-and-culture/eddie-vedder-helps -u2-celebrate-joshua-tree-during-bands-first-us-show-trump-era.

Rock Express. 1987. "Looking for the Soul of America." *Rock Express*, April 1.

Rose, Charlie. 2016. Interview with Bono. *Charlie Rose*. PBS.

Scott, Eugene. 2016. "Bono: Trump 'Potentially the Worst Idea That Ever Happened to America.'" *CNN*, September 21.

Shaikh, Amad. 2019. "Remembering 9/11 as a Muslim American." *Al Jazeera English*, September 11. https://www.aljazeera.com/indepth/opinion/ 2011/09/20119893039787215.html.

Stockman, Steve. 2003. *Walk On: The Spiritual Journey of U2*. Lake Mary, FL: Relevant Books.

Stokes, Niall. 1987. "The World About Us." *Hot Press*, March 26.

———. 2001. *Into the Heart: The Stories Behind Every U2 Song*. New York, NY: Thunder's Mouth Press.

———. 2017. "U2: The Stories Behind Their Greatest Songs." *Hot Press*. July 18.

Sutcliffe-Braithwaite, Florence, and Natalie Thomlinson. 2018. "Review of 'Britain and the End of Coal, National Women Against Pit Closures: Gender, Trade Unionism and Community Activism in the Miners' Strike, 1984–5.'" *Contemporary British History* 32 (1): 78–100.

"The Enduring Chill." *Propaganda*, Issue 4. December 1, 1986.

The Joshua Tree Tour 2017. *U2.Com* (blog). January 5. https://www.u2.com/news/ title/the-joshua-tree-tour-2017.

"'The Joshua Tree.'" *Propaganda*, Issue 5. January 1, 1987.

The Rock and Roll Hall of Fame, and Newseum. n.d. *Louder Than Words: Rock, Power & Politics*. Museum Exhibit.

The Southern Poverty Law Center. 2020. "Review of Family Separation under the Trump Administration—a Timeline.'" The Southern Poverty Law Center. https://www.splcenter.org/news/2020/06/17/family-separation-under -trump-administration-timeline.

Thrills, Adrian. 1987. "Cactus World View." *New Musical Express*, March 14.

Time. 1987. "U2: Rock's Hottest Ticket." *Time*, April 27.

Toronto Star. 1987. "Trio Gives U2 Raad-ical Strings." *Toronto Star*, March 20.

Travis, Alan. 2014. "Thatcher Was to Call Labour and Miners 'Enemy within' in Abandoned Speech." *The Guardian*, October 2. https://www.theguardian.com/politics/2014/oct/03/thatcher-labour-miners-enemy-within-brighton-bomb.

Trebe, Ann. 1991. "On Trial in Killing of 'Sister Sam' Star." *USA Today*, October 23.

Trump, Donald. 2020. "2020 State of the Union Address." Presented at the 2020 State of the Union Address, February 4.

Turner, Steve. 2001. *Imagine: A Vision for Christians in the Arts*. Downers Grove, IL: IVP Books

2CR FM. 2000. Bono Interview. November 18.

US Department of Health and Human Services. 2019. *Care Provider Facilities Described Challenges Addressing Mental Health Needs of Children in HHS Custody*. Edited by Joanna M. Chiedi. Office of Inspector General. https://perma.cc/2RPJ-WM5H.

U2, The Joshua Tree Tour 2017, music and lyrics by U2, live performance, Stadio Olimpico, Rome, July 16.

———. The Joshua Tree Tour 2017, music and lyrics by U2, live performance, Ford Field, Detroit, September 3.

———. *Songs of Innocence*. Interscope Records B0022124-02, 2014, compact disc liner notes.

———. *The Joshua Tree: 20th Anniversary Remaster*. Island Records, Interscope Records, Ume B0010286-02, 2007, compact disc liner notes.

———. U2 Tours—Full List. @U2. https://www.atu2.com/tours/tour/.

Varga, George. 2017. "U2 Revisits 'Joshua Tree' Album 30 Years Later on Tour, While Finishing New Album." *The San Diego Union-Tribune*, September 20. https://www.sandiegouniontribune.com/entertainment/music/sd-et-music-u2-preview-20170920-story.html.

Waters, John. 1994. *Race of Angels: The Genesis of U2*. London, UK: Fourth Estate.

Wawzenek, Bryan. 2016. "How A Tragic Death Inspired U2's 'One Tree Hill': The Story Behind Every 'Joshua Tree' Song." *Diffuser.Fm* (blog). July 3.

———. 2017. "U2 Gets Cinematic On 'Where the Streets Have No Name': The Story Behind Every 'Joshua Tree' Song." *Diffuser.Fm* (blog). February 28.

———. 2017. "U2 Goes Minimalist on 'With or Without You': The Story Behind Every 'Joshua Tree' Song." *Diffuser.Fm* (blog). March 2.

———. 2017. "U2 Honors the 'Mothers of the Disappeared': The Story Behind Every 'Joshua Tree' Song." *Diffuser.Fm* (blog). March 10. https://diffuser.fm/u2-mothers-of-the-disappeared/.

———. 2017. "U2 Updates The Gospel On 'I Still Haven't Found What I'm Looking For': The Story Behind Every 'Joshua Tree' Song." *Diffuser.Fm* (blog). March 1.

Wenner, Jann S. 2005. "Bono: The Rolling Stone Interview." *Rolling Stone*, November 3. https://www.rollingstone.com/music/music-news/bono-the-rolling-stone-interview-75927/.

———. 2017. "Bono: The Rolling Stone Interview." *Rolling Stone*, December 27. https://www.rollingstone.com/music/music-features/bono-the-rolling-stone-interview-3-203774/.

White, Timothy. 1987. *Timothy White's Rock Stars*. June 1.

"With or Without You: Bono Bans Donald Trump from Tour." *RTÉ*, May 16. https://www.rte.ie/entertainment/2017/0516/875466-bono-bans-donald-trump/.

INDEX

Permissions

Grateful acknowledgment is made to the following for permission to use both published and unpublished materials:

Apple Inc.: Quotes from Bono from the July 20, 2017, Beats 1 Radio interview "U2: *Joshua Tree* 30th Anniversary Interview | Apple Music" at https://www.youtube.com/watch?v=vsKZ3YrF_3Q. Courtesy Beats 1, Apple Music.

Penguin Random House, LLC: Excerpts from *Bono: In Conversation with Michka Assayas* by Michka Assayas, Riverhead Books. Reprinted with permission.

Mother Jones: Excerpts from "Bono Bites Back," by Adam Block, from *Mother Jones* magazine, May 1989. Reprinted with permission.

National Public Radio: Quote from Bono from the March 20, 2017, interview with Steve Inskeep on *Morning Edition*, NPR, "U2 on *The Joshua Tree*, a Lasting Ode to a Divided America," at https://www.npr.org/2017/03/20/520443744/u2-on-the-joshua-tree-a-lasting-ode-to-a-divided-america. Courtesy NPR.

Smithsonian Enterprises: Excerpts from "The Original Meanings of the 'American Dream' and 'America First' Were Starkly Different from How We Use Them Today," by Anna Diamond, from *Smithsonian* magazine. Copyright 2018 Smithsonian Institution. All rights reserved. Reprinted with permission from Smithsonian Enterprises. Any reproduction in any medium is strictly prohibited without permission from Smithsonian magazine.